Quartet

Quartet

Student's Book 1

Françoise Grellet
Alan Maley
Wim Welsing

with a contribution from
Norman Coe

Oxford
University
Press

Oxford University Press
Walton Street, Oxford OX2 6DP

London Glasgow New York Toronto
Delhi Bombay Calcutta Madras Karachi
Kuala Lumpur Singapore Hong Kong Tokyo
Nairobi Dar Es Salaam Cape Town
Melbourne Auckland

and associated companies in
Beirut Berlin Ibadan Mexico City Nicosia

OXFORD is a trade mark of Oxford University
Press

ISBN 0 19 433580 1 (Student's Book 1)
ISBN 0 19 433581 X (Teacher's Book 1)
ISBN 0 19 433582 8 (2 Cassettes 1)

Composition in Helvetica by
Filmtype Services Limited
Scarborough, North Yorkshire

Printed in Hong Kong

Recording produced by Peter Menzies

Illustrations by   Phil Green
                    Ed McLachlan
                    Jim Robins

Photographs by Dafydd Jones

The publisher would like to thank the following for
permission to use photographs, and pictures:

Aerofilms
Arts Council of Great Britain
Barnaby's Picture Library
George Behrend
City of Birmingham Publicity Department
Camera Press
Douglas Dickens
Dr. A.A. J.J. v.d. Eerden
Nick Hedges
John Hillelson Agency
Oxford Mail and Times
Pix Features
Popperfoto
Royal Commonwealth Society for the Blind
Teylers Stichting Haarlem
Thames Valley Police

Contents

1
Kidnapped

1 Read this newspaper article carefully. Then complete the map on the next page.

EVENING HERALD MONDAY, 4TH MARCH

BANK DIRECTOR KIDNAPPED

THIS MORNING, in an obviously well planned operation, Sir Anthony Blything was kidnapped in Kennington Park in South London. Sir Anthony is Managing Director of the British Overseas Bank and one of Britain's wealthiest men. So far nothing has been heard from the kidnappers, but police believe that money may well be the motive for the crime.

55-year-old Sir Anthony, who lives in a large house in Kennington, has always been a keen sportsman. 'He always likes to keep fit,' said his chauffeur. 'Every morning at 7.30 sharp I drive him to Kennington Park for his morning run. I stand at the gate with a stop-watch, and time him. He runs half a mile in about four and a half minutes, which is very good for a man of his age. This morning he passed the half-way point in 2 minutes 10 seconds.'

But Sir Anthony never completed his run. His chauffeur did not see what happened, but other people have reported seeing Sir Anthony being pushed into a green van. One eye-witness said, 'I was taking my dog for a walk. There was a young man and a woman near a van. It looked like a Council van and I didn't take much notice of them. A bit further on this man in shorts ran past me. When I was almost at the swimming-pool I heard a shout. I looked round and saw the young man and woman pushing the man in shorts into the van. Then they drove away. It all happened so quickly, it seems like a dream.'

The police immediately set up road-blocks on major roads leading out of London, but so far there is no trace of the van or of Sir Anthony.

Our Labour Correspondent writes: The British Overseas Bank was recently in the news when a six-week strike resulted in the dismissal of ten bank employees.

a Indicate on the map where the chauffeur (C) was standing.
b Indicate the direction of Sir Anthony's run. (Use arrows.)
c Indicate where the following people were at the time of the kidnapping:
   the kidnappers (K), Sir Anthony (A), and the man with the dog (M).

When you have finished, compare your plan with your partner.

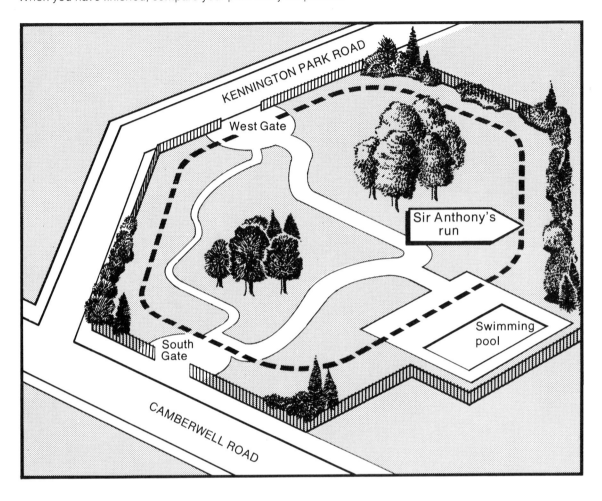

2   Listen to the news report on the tape, and then, from the following photos, choose the one that fits the description of the man and the one that fits the description of the woman. When you have finished, compare your ideas with your partner.

This is Radio 4. Here is the seven o'clock news for Monday the 4th of March.

Early this morning Sir Anthony Blything, Managing Director of the British Overseas Bank, was kidnapped. He was having his usual morning run in Kennington Park when he was stopped at gun-point by a young man and a woman and forced into a small van which immediately drove away. This afternoon a van which police say is the one used by the kidnappers was found in a back street not far from Kennington Park. The van had been stolen. Police wish to interview two people in connection with the kidnapping. Their descriptions are as follows: a man aged about 25, of medium height and heavily built; he has a roundish face, short dark hair and prominent ears; a woman aged about 20, tall and slim with long blonde hair and pointed features.

Anyone who can give information should ring New Scotland Yard or contact their local police-station.

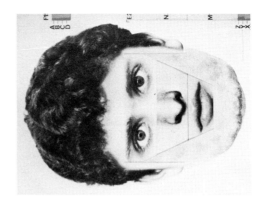

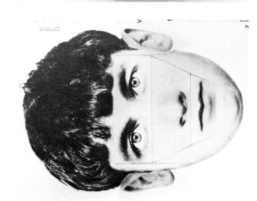

3

3 The following is the interview between the police and a witness.

This interview led to the police description which was broadcast in the radio news. Work with a partner, and complete the policeman's questions.

Policeman ....?
Witness About 25, I suppose.
Policeman ....?
Witness No, not really tall. But not short, either. I'd say middling.
Policeman ....?
Witness Not fat nor thin, really. But he certainly looked strong, you know, like a boxer or something.

Policeman ....?
Witness Well, sort of roundish, as far as I can remember. And he had short hair.
Policeman ....?
Witness Dark.
Policeman ....?
Witness Let me think … umm … oh, yes. He had ears that stuck out.
Policeman Well, thanks very much. You've been most helpful.

When you have finished, listen to the actual conversation on the tape and compare it with your version.

4 On Tuesday, the day after the kidnapping, Lady Blything received a recorded message. Listen to it carefully and make notes of all the things that Lady Blything must do to satisfy the kidnappers.

When you have finished, compare your notes with your partner.

5 On Tuesday morning a note addressed to Lady Blything was found blowing along County Street, not far from Kennington Park. It seemed to have been written by Sir Anthony and dropped out of a window. However, since it was windy, it was not clear exactly which building it had come from. The message was in code, but the police quickly understood it. Can you?

To Lady Blything, Victoria House, Clover Square, Kennington

JV ABXO JXOV

F EXSB YBBK HFAKXMMBA YV X VLRKD JXK XKA TLJXK.

TB XOB FK X CIXQ LK QEB QLM CILLO LC X EFDE

YRFIAFKD. TB AFA KLQ AOFSB CXO QL DBQ EBOB.

QEBV EXSB DRKP YRQ BSBOVQEFKD TFII YB XII OFDEQ

FC VLR DFSB QEBJ QEB JLKBV. ALKQ TLOOV.

XII JV ILSB

XKQELKV

6.1 This is an extract from a long documentary article about the kidnapping in a Sunday newspaper. Read it carefully.

When Detective Inspector Croft talked to Lady Blything on Tuesday evening, she confirmed that the coded message was from her husband, and that he wanted her to pay the money. 'We often leave messages for each other in a simple code when we don't want the children to understand,' she explained.

Croft told Lady Blything that the police were secretly watching all the big blocks of flats on County Street, the road where the message was found. 'We don't know exactly which block of flats it is,' said the Inspector. 'It was quite windy this morning, so we can't tell which block the message was dropped from. In any case, we don't want to go into any of the flats at the moment because that might endanger your husband,' the Inspector went on.

'I quite understand, and I think we should all be very careful,' said Lady Blything.

'Exactly,' replied the Inspector. 'In fact, if you agree to pay the money, we will not move until your daughter and husband are both safe.'

'I'm very worried that something might happen to my daughter,' Lady Blything confessed, 'but I suppose I'll have to do exactly as they say.'

'Good,' said the Inspector. 'If you follow the instructions, now that we know more or less which house it is, I don't think we'll have any problems. And I even hope we'll get the money back.'

6.2 The next day one newspaper carried this short item. In what way does this newspaper version differ from what really took place? Compare your answer with your partner.

WEDNESDAY, 15 MARCH

LATE NEWS

In connection with the disappearance of Sir Anthony Blything, a CID officer, Detective Inspector Croft, had a meeting with Lady Blything yesterday afternoon. A CID spokesman said later that Lady Blything was willing to provide the money demanded by the kidnappers. Inspector Croft explained to Lady Blything that the police so far had no idea where the kidnappers had taken Sir Anthony, although they believed that he was still in London. Lady Blything pointed out that she was most concerned for the safety of her husband and her daughter, and she specially asked that the police should not try to stop the kidnappers or to interfere with the handing over of the money. Croft agreed that the police would make no move until Sir Anthony and their daughter were both safe.

7 The police made very careful arrangements for the day when the money was going to be collected. The idea was to follow the route taken by the kidnappers, without sending a car after them.

You are in the control room of New Scotland Yard. On your map you have the positions of the policemen and policewomen – none of them in uniform, of course – who are going to report the route of the car. Now listen to the tape. Note the route of the car on your map. When you have finished check your results with your partner.

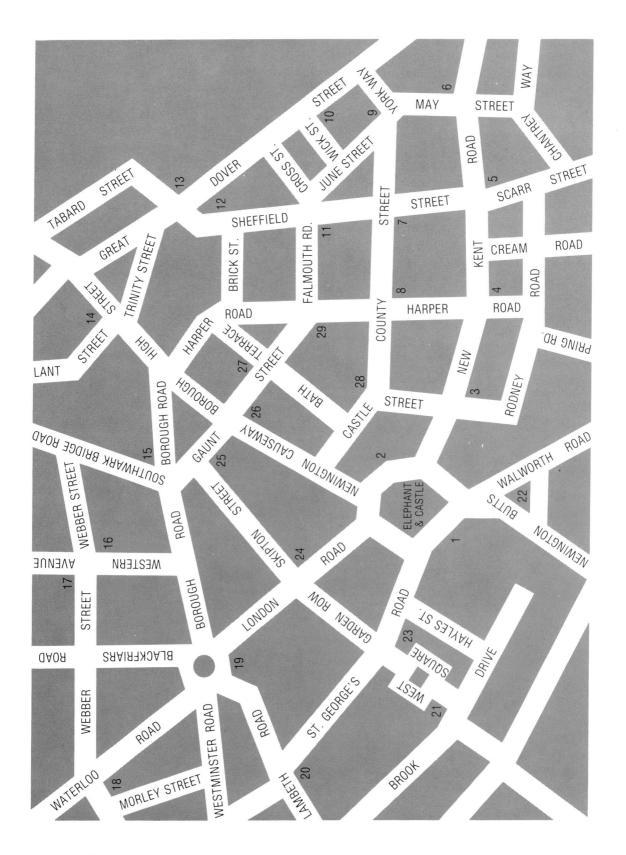

8 Groups of armed police were placed at the ends of County Street and also behind number 36, the block of flats where Sir Anthony was being held. But the police did not want to make the first move; they realized that the kidnappers would soon want to make their escape, and the police were prepared to wait.

Throughout the day nothing happened. The police waited and watched, but with growing impatience. Lady Blything, waiting at home with her daughter, was also anxious for news, but she too had to wait. Detective Inspector Croft guessed – rightly – that the kidnappers were waiting for the evening, when it would be dark.

At seven o'clock it began to get dark, and by half past eight it was already night. Still nothing happened. Then, just before nine o'clock, above the noise of the traffic, something else could be heard: a helicopter. It landed briefly on the top of number 36 County Street, and, before the police could decide what to do, it rose and disappeared into the night sky.

The police now rushed into the building. In a top-floor flat they found Sir Anthony tied to a chair, but in good health and very pleased to see the police.

The kidnappers were never caught. But about a year later the ten strikers who were dismissed from the British Overseas Bank each received a registered parcel. Every parcel contained £9,500 in used five-pound notes, and a message that said .... .

What do you think the message said? (Remember that the ransom was £100,000.) Write it down, then compare it with your partner.

9 Read this passage from Robert Louis Stevenson's *Kidnapped*.

It was the last I saw. Already strong hands had been plucking me back from the ship's side; and now a thunderbolt seemed to strike me; I saw a great flash of fire, and fell senseless.

I came to myself in darkness, in great pain, bound hand and foot, and deafened by many unfamiliar noises. There sounded in my ears a roaring of water as of a huge milldam, the thrashing of heavy sprays, the thundering of the sails, and the shrill cries of seamen. The whole world now heaved giddily up, and now rushed giddily downward; and so sick and hurt was I in body, and my mind so much confounded, that it took me a long while, chasing my thoughts up and down, and ever stunned again by a fresh stab of pain, to realize that I must be lying somewhere bound in the belly of that unlucky ship, and that the wind must have strengthened to a gale. With the clear perception of my plight, there fell upon me a blackness of despair, a horror of remorse at my own folly, and a passion of anger at my uncle, that once more bereft me of my senses.

When I returned again to life, the same uproar, the same confused and violent movements, shook and deafened me; and presently, to my other pains and distresses, there was added the sickness of an unused landsman on the sea. In that time of my adventurous youth, I suffered many hardships; but none that was so crushing to my mind and body, or lit by so few hopes, as these first hours aboard the brig.

I heard a gun fire, and supposed the storm had proved too strong for us, and we were firing signals of distress. The thought of deliverance, even by death in the deep sea, was welcome to me. Yet it was no such matter; but (as I was afterwards told) a common habit of the captain's, which I here set down to show that even the worst man may have his kindlier side. We were then passing, it appeared, within some miles of Dysart, where the brig was built, and where old Mrs. Hoseason, the captain's mother, had come some years before to live; and whether outward or inward bound, the *Covenant* was never suffered to go by that place by day, without a gun fired and colours shown.

I had no measure of time; day and night were alike in that ill-smelling cavern of the ship's bowels where I lay; and the misery of my situation drew out the hours to double. How long, therefore, I lay waiting to hear the ship split upon some rock, or to feel her reel headforemost into the depths of the sea, I have not the means of computation. But sleep at length stole from me the consciousness of sorrow.

I was wakened by the light of a hand-lantern shining in my face. A small man of about thirty, with green eyes and a tangle of fair hair, stood looking down at me.

2
Games and sports

1.1 You will probably be familiar with the following games: soccer, tennis, baseball, ice-hockey. Which description fits which game?

| 1 | soccer (association football) | A | A game played on a field with bases, with a bat and ball, by two teams of nine players each. |

| 2 | tennis | B | A game played on ice with angled sticks and a rubber disc (puck), by two teams of six players each wearing skates. |

| 3 | baseball (national game of U.S.) | C | A game played on a large field with a round inflated leather ball, by two teams of eleven players each. |

| 4 | ice-hockey | D | A game played on a court, by two or four players who hit a ball backwards and forwards across a net. |

Match them here.

1	2	3	4

1.2 Here are some details about eight other games. Can you give a description of some of them in the same way as above?

name of game	some details			description
	location	equipment	players	
table-tennis (ping-pong)	on a table	bats and ball	2 or 4 players	
Rugby League (allowing professionals) Rugby Union (only amateurs)	on a large field	oval-shaped inflated leather ball, which may be kicked or handled	2 teams of 13 players each 2 teams of 15 players each	
badminton	on an area smaller than a tennis-court with a high, narrow net in the middle	rackets and shuttlecocks	2 or 4 players	
cricket	on a grass field	bats and wickets and a hard ball	2 teams of 11 players each	
golf	a golf-course (golf-links); a stretch of land with a series of 9 or 18 holes on smooth greens	a small hard ball and a set of clubs of different shapes and sizes for each player	2 or 4 players	
basket-ball	an area larger than a tennis-court, with an open-ended net fixed 10 ft above the ground on both sides	a large inflated ball	2 teams of 5 players each	
hockey	a large field	long curved sticks and a hard ball	2 teams of 11 players each	

1.3 Can you give a description and some details of a (national) game not mentioned here?

name of game	some details			description
	location	equipment	players	

2 A guessing game

Look at the photographs and diagrams on pages 10, 11 and 12. Choose one of the people in action, but do not say whom you have in mind.

Your partner may ask you seven questions about this person (for example about the way he/she is dressed, what he/she has in his/her hands or where he/she is playing). If your partner has guessed the right photograph and the name of the game, and has matched the photograph with the diagram, he/she scores a point. If not, you score a point yourself. Next it is your partner's turn to choose a photograph. You may not ask more than five questions, and so on. With the third photograph not more than three questions may be asked, and with the fourth not more than two. The following expressions may be useful:

So it must be …	*playing … .*
It can't be anyone but …	*on … .*
It can only be …	

1

3

2

4

5

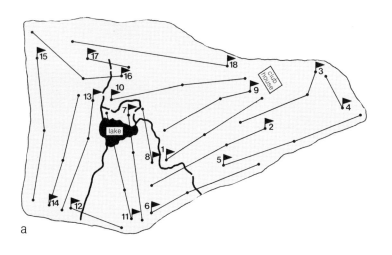

a

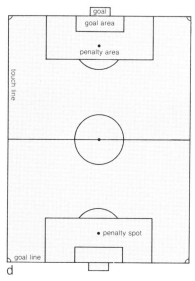

d

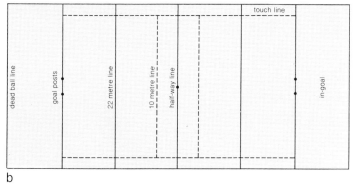

b

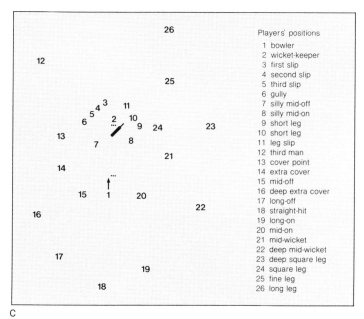

Players' positions

1 bowler
2 wicket-keeper
3 first slip
4 second slip
5 third slip
6 gully
7 silly mid-off
8 silly mid-on
9 short leg
10 short leg
11 leg slip
12 third man
13 cover point
14 extra cover
15 mid-off
16 deep extra cover
17 long-off
18 straight-hit
19 long-on
20 mid-on
21 mid-wicket
22 deep mid-wicket
23 deep square leg
24 square leg
25 fine leg
26 long leg

c

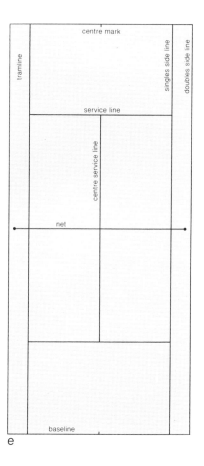

e

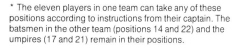

* The eleven players in one team can take any of these
positions according to instructions from their captain. The
batsmen in the other team (positions 14 and 22) and the
umpires (17 and 21) remain in their positions.

3 Have a look at the other sports mentioned below in alphabetical order.

Can you show which you enjoy watching and which not, which you would not mind taking part in, which you think involve too many risks and which you think violent or aggressive? Tick off the appropriate boxes.

Next compare your opinions with those of the members of your group. What do the majority of your group think?

sports	you					majority of group					Anna and Nigel				
	enjoy watching	hate watching	don't mind taking part in	think too risky	think violent/aggressive	enjoy watching	hate watching	don't mind taking part in	think too risky	think violent/aggressive	enjoy watching	hate watching	don't mind taking part in	think too risky	think violent/aggressive
aerobatics															
athletics															
bobsleighing															
boxing															
bull-fighting															
canoeing															
car-racing															
cycling															
fencing															
gliding															
horse-racing															
mountaineering															
rodeo riding															
sailing															
skating															
ski-jumping															
skiing (crosscountry)															
swimming															
wrestling															

4 Now listen to the conversation between Anna and Nigel. Can you complete the third column by putting their initials in the appropriate boxes?

5.1 In recent years the amount of violence on and around the soccer field has increased. A number of supporters seem to enjoy playing a more active role than just watching the game. The following is a newspaper article about the events that took place when England played Belgium in the European Championship in Italy in June 1980. Who does the reporter blame: the players, the managers, the television and radio commentators, the Italian police, or …?

DAILY EXPRESS, Friday June 13 1980

ENGLISH FANS IN TEAR-GAS RIOT

Match is halted as police charge onto terraces

TEAR-gas fired by police to quell rioting England fans halted a Soccer international in Turin last night.

England goalkeeper Ray Clemence was led from the field with eyes streaming as the gas drifted across the field from the terraces.

Manager Ron Greenwood asked the German referee to stop the European Championship match with Belgium three minutes before half-time.

Play resumed four minutes later after Clemence had received treatment from the England trainer.

The fighting broke out in the 29th minute when Belgium scored an equalizing goal to make the score 1–1.

Running battles

Gangs of English supporters among the crowd attacked groups of neutral Italians standing near them in the Stadio Communale.

Italian police wearing helmets moved in, swinging batons. And tear-gas shells exploded behind Clemence's goal.

Later, with running battles still going on, a message from Mr Greenwood was broadcast over the public address system.

He told the fans: 'You are doing the chances of the team no good and the reputation of England no good. Please, please, behave yourselves.'

Millions of TV viewers watching at home heard former England star and BBC commentator Bobby Charlton say: 'I am certainly not proud to be British right now.'

Football Association Press Officer Glenn Kirton said England had sold only 4,500 tickets to members of their official travel club.

'But the Italians are selling tickets at the turnstiles, so we have virtually no control over who comes in wearing red, white and blue,' he said.

'The Swiss observer for UEFA will obviously have to make a report and, in the extreme, England could be banned from the competition.'

England captain Kevin Keegan said: 'For 10 minutes we were all so proud that our fans had made the journey. Now I am ashamed to be English.

'I know 95 per cent of our followers are great, but the rest are just drunks.'

© Daily Express

5.2 **The facts**

What is the order in which the various events took place according to the *Daily Express*? Which passage or phrase tells you? Use the left side of the table below to take down your findings. The right side of the table will be reserved for checking the facts reported against the information given in another article, in the *Daily Mail*. Compare your findings with those of the other members of your group. This is the list of the events:

a The police take action.
b Goalkeeper Ray Clemence is treated.
c The game is stopped.
d The game is started again.
e The fighting breaks out.
f Ron Greenwood addresses the fans.
g England scores (1–0).
h Belgium scores (1–1).

<table>
<tr><td colspan="3">The Daily Express article:
ENGLISH FANS IN TEAR-GAS RIOT</td><td colspan="4">The Daily Mail article:
HOOLIGANS SHAME ENGLAND</td></tr>
<tr><td>order in which events take place</td><td>events (list a–h)</td><td>passage or phrase that contains information on order in which events take place</td><td colspan="4">Are the nature of the events and the times mentioned in the Daily Express article confirmed by the Daily Mail?</td></tr>
<tr><td></td><td></td><td></td><td>yes *</td><td>no *</td><td colspan="2">which passage/phrase tells you?</td></tr>
<tr><td>1</td><td></td><td></td><td></td><td></td><td colspan="2"></td></tr>
<tr><td>2</td><td></td><td></td><td></td><td></td><td colspan="2"></td></tr>
<tr><td>3</td><td></td><td></td><td></td><td></td><td colspan="2"></td></tr>
<tr><td>4</td><td></td><td></td><td></td><td></td><td colspan="2"></td></tr>
<tr><td>5</td><td></td><td></td><td></td><td></td><td colspan="2"></td></tr>
<tr><td>6</td><td></td><td></td><td></td><td></td><td colspan="2"></td></tr>
<tr><td>7</td><td></td><td></td><td></td><td></td><td colspan="2"></td></tr>
<tr><td>8</td><td></td><td></td><td></td><td></td><td colspan="2"></td></tr>
</table>

*tick off the appropriate box

5.3 Read the article 'Hooligans shame England' from the *Daily Mail*. Does the author confirm the *Daily Express* report? Use the right side of the table above. Compare your findings with other members of your group.

Hooligans shame England

From JEFF POWELL in Turin

ITALIAN riot police baton-charged and tear-gassed England's army of football hooligans to bloody defeat in Turin last night.

The penalty for another nauseating outbreak of mob violence may be England's suspension from future European competition.

The first match of England's assault on the current European championship had to be held up for five minutes as the blinding effect of the tear-gas was sponged from the players' eyes.

The battle on the terraces of Turin's Stadio Communale raged on.

There are fears for the life of one fan who plunged head first into the empty concrete moat surrounding the pitch.

Only the worst of the wounded were taken to hospital. In their disgust with the English, the authorities had many others dragged out and piled into an unconscious heap in the gutter.

That is precisely where England's reputation as a nation lies this morning.

No one feels more humiliated than the players, whose chances of winning world football's second-biggest prize receded into a nervous, distracted 1–1 draw with Belgium.

England's manager Ron Greenwood who had to appeal from the touchline for the game to be stopped because his goalkeeper, Ray Clemence, could barely see, said: 'I want nothing to do with that lot. I hope they put them in a big boat and drop them in the ocean half-way back.

Baton-waving Italian riot police move in as English fans try to escape across the pitch barrier

'I am ashamed of people like that. They shouldn't be allowed at football. The Italians must think we're idiots. I'm proud of my profession but they make me disgusted.'

The trouble erupted when Belgium equalized an early goal by England's Ray Wilkins, after half an hour of play.

The Belgians and English fans had been segregated into opposite ends of the ground so the hooligan element in the Union Jack section turned on groups of Italians.

The police immediately went in, swinging batons, cracking heads and added blood to the drink which was already defiling the Union Jacks draped around the young thugs behind England's goal.

As one group of troublemakers was cornered, another mob led by skinheads charged the police. They were repulsed by a full-scale baton charge. The terrace was virtually cleared by tear-gas canisters fired into the heaving crowd.

But not before the giant electric score-board on top of the terrace had been knocked out of action.

The match stopped as clouds of smoke and fumes blew across the field. Clemence and two other England players were taken to the covered benches for treatment.

Blinded

Colour TV close-ups showed them with streaming eyes, retching, coughing and gasping for breath.

The West German referee ran round in circles, hands over his eyes. The linesmen appeared to be blinded.

Men with buckets of water and sponges splashed players' faces.

Greenwood had an appeal broadcast for calm during play at the start of the second half. He said 'Please will you behave yourselves. You are doing the chances of the England team and the reputation of England no good at all. Please, please stay calm for the rest of your stay.'

Unhappily, most such appeals in the past to whatever remains of the mob's common sense, have been in vain.

6 Now look at some of the details given in the two articles.

6.1 **The rioters**

The people who caused the violence are disapproved of in both articles. Which article used the following descriptions? (Tick off the appropriate boxes.)

	Daily Express	Daily Mail
rioting English fans	☐	☐
England's army of football hooligans	☐	☐
young thugs	☐	☐
trouble-makers	☐	☐
mob	☐	☐

6.2 **The appeal made by the England manager**

Ron Greenwood's appeal to the rioting fans is quoted in both articles. Are there any important differences between the two versions? In fact he made two requests. Complete the sentences:

a Please, will you … .
b Please, please, stay … .

What would you say about the form of these requests? Tick off the appropriate boxes.

		a	b
They are:	polite	☐	☐
	impolite	☐	☐
	strong	☐	☐
	weak	☐	☐

6.3 **The police**

Collect the details given about the police in the two articles.

nationality	sort of police	equipment	activities

6.4 **The results of the battle**

Make notes from the two articles about the various people affected.

People affected.	What were their symptoms or what was their behaviour?	Who or what was the cause?	How were they treated?
Ray Clemence	*eyes streaming*	*tear-gas*	*led from the field*

6.5 Comments given by various people

Complete the table below with one or two key words for each question.

	How did each of them feel?	Why did they feel this way?
Kevin Keegan		
Bobby Charlton		
players		
Ron Greenwood		

6.6 The two articles compared

			Daily Express	Daily Mail
The facts	a	All the important facts are given.	☐	☐
	b	Enough important facts are given to get a good picture of what happened.	☐	☐
	c	Not enough important facts are given.	☐	☐
The details	a	Most details given add valuable information.	☐	☐
	b	Most details given are interesting, but not really necessary.	☐	☐
	c	Most details given are unnecessary.	☐	☐
The author's intention	a	He tries to give a full account without showing personal feelings.	☐	☐
	b	He tries to tell the truth but is not afraid of showing personal feelings.	☐	☐
	c	He is especially interested in telling the readers what he himself felt when watching all this violence.	☐	☐
I/we think	a	The article is very well written.	☐	☐
	b	The article is reasonably well written.	☐	☐
	c	It is a boring article.	☐	☐

7 Choose one of the following assignments.

a Imagine you are the Swiss observer for UEFA. Write his report about the events during the soccer match between England and Belgium in Turin. It is important for UEFA to have the facts: Who did what? who are responsible? and so on. The observer may of course add some personal recommendations.

b Write a short letter to Ray Clemence. You may feel sorry about what happened to him and you understand his anger, but you feel worried about the suggestion he made to put the rioters in a boat and drop them in the ocean. Point out why this sort of reaction will not really solve any problems.

c Imagine you are one of the many well-meaning fans of the English national team. Can you write a short leaflet to be handed out to all fans before the next international match? You may use parts of the articles and also illustrate the text with drawings. (Most fans will not want to spend too much time reading it.)

3
Rescue

1   On July 2nd some inhabitants of an island in the Pacific found the following letter in a bottle on the beach.

I am sending this letter in a bottle hoping it may reach someone soon. If anyone finds it, please contact my wife, 11 Dorset Drive, Winchester, England. I'm on an island which I think is uninhabited, but I am not sure as it looks fairly large. It may take several days to explore it all. I am not sure where I am exactly, but I will try to explain.

We had a good flight to San Francisco, but after that we went through a bad storm, there was a strange noise in the engine, and we were asked to fasten our seat-belts. We were about two hours from Australia and we were rather tired after such a long time in the plane, so I am afraid I must have fallen asleep. After that, I can't remember very much. When I woke up, we were going down fast and quite suddenly, the sea was very near. There must be several islands around here: I remember flying low over some of them. Then there was a terrific bump as the plane hit the water, and I was knocked unconscious. When I woke up, I was floating on the water, strapped to my seat.... I suppose it saved my life.... all the others had disappeared. I should have tried to swim back and look but I was exhausted, and I had probably drifted away as there was no sign of the aeroplane anywhere nearby.

I managed to reach this island, but not without great difficulty as much of the coast is rocky and there are a great many reefs. I will now try to explore the island, but all there seems to be on it is thick jungle except for what looks like a fairly high mountain a few miles away, right in the middle of the island. I can perhaps try to live here on fruit for a while, and then build a raft. But where can I go? I cannot see any other island in the distance.... I wish I had some bright clothes that I could use as a signal, but with this dense jungle I am not sure it would be any good.

If only this letter could reach someone.... I never thought I would ever have to send a message this way. Just as people do in books. But if there's only one chance in a thousand, it's worth trying.

                                 Peter Wrightson

(You can also contact the people in charge of the seminar I was going to attend: Bromflex Corporation, Int., 17, Bullfinch Road, Sydney, Australia.)

1.1 What facts do you know about Peter Wrightson from this message? How do you think he filled in the following disembarkation card when boarding his plane? Try to complete it yourself. Do not worry if some of the information is missing.

DISEMBARKATION CARD

Surname .... First name(s) ....

Date of birth ....

Permanent address ....

Profession ....

Port of embarkation ....

Port of disembarkation .... Via ....

Reason for journey ....

Destination address ....

Passport number ....

1.2 Peter Wrightson's letter was found on a neighbouring island. Here is a map of the group of islands where he is. Can you tell which of these islands he is on? (Visibility at sea is not more than ten miles.) Compare your ideas with a partner.

Santa Barbara islands

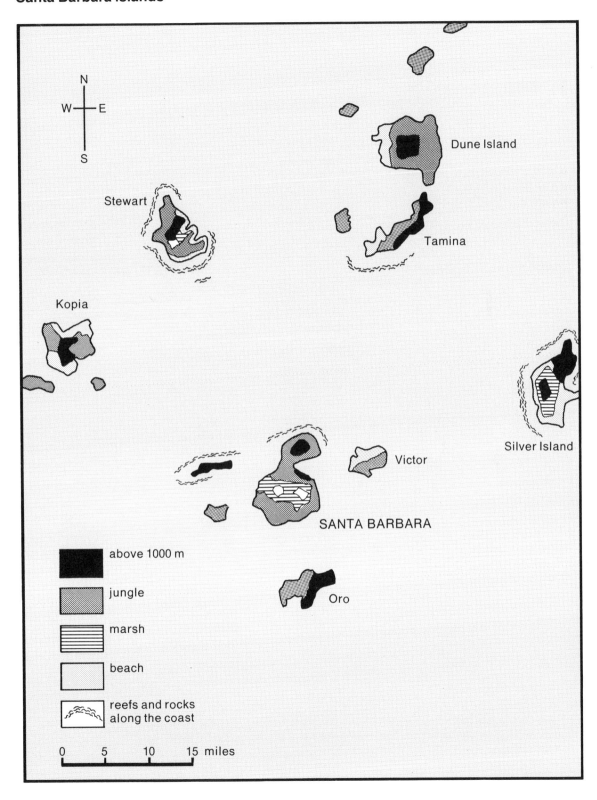

N
W—E
S

Dune Island

Stewart

Tamina

Kopia

Silver Island

Victor

SANTA BARBARA

■ above 1000 m

▨ jungle

▤ marsh

▦ beach

〜 reefs and rocks
along the coast

Oro

0   5   10   15 miles

1.3 Read the message again. Can you find some expressions used to convey hope and regret?

Can you think of some more expressions of this kind? What else do you think Peter Wrightson regrets?

2 Surviving on a desert island

Survival is often a question of luck (how soon will you be seen and rescued?), or of physical fitness.

In the following table, a number of dangers have been listed. Can you decide for each of them:
- what can be done to prevent them or fight against them?
- how this can be done?
- what is needed to do this?

Can you then add to the list of dangers?

dangers	precautions	methods	instruments needed	qualities needed
cold	fire/sun clothes	taking advantage of the sun making a fire using animal furs/plants for clothes	mirror weapons a needle	perseverance courage
hunger				
wild animals				
illness				
	If ..., then you won't ... . You could ... . A ... will keep you from	By ..., you could	In order to ... ... will be necessary. With a ... you can ... . If you have a ... you can	You have to be ... to ... . You'd need a lot of ... in order to ... .

First, complete the table on your own. When you have finished, discuss what you have decided with a partner. The expressions you will find at the bottom of each column should help you.

3 The survival kit

All of these items mentioned in the first column below can be fitted into a small tin and be ready for use at any time.

3.1 Can you match the items with the pictures and the description of their use? Do it on your own first. Then check with a partner.

A a knife
B matches
C a compass
D a pencil
E a plastic bag
F aluminium foil (1.5 m)
G a small mirror
H fish-hooks
I a candle
J a large needle
K antiseptic cream
L water purification tablets
M two bright-orange balloons
N 30 m or more of strong thread
O a pad of thin paper
P sticking plasters
Q a large piece of nylon material
R a whistle

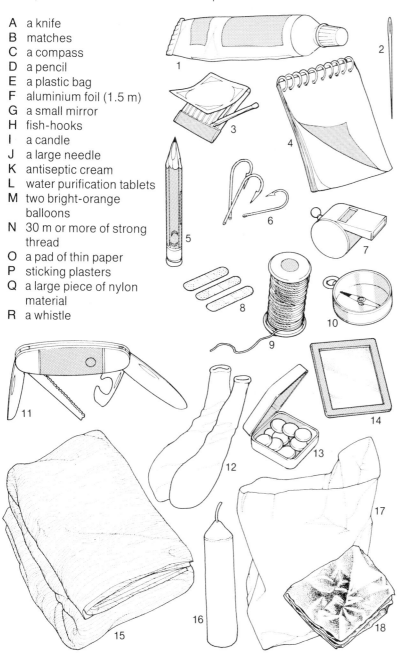

a To carry or store food or water.
b To be used for signalling or protecting the face from sand or dust. Can also help to filter dirty water.
c To cut branches or defend oneself.
d To catch fish for food.
e To assist rescue parties by leaving notes.
f For making and repairing clothes.
g To set traps to catch animals, build shelters, repair clothes, etc.
h To light fires.
i To find your way more easily and quickly when there is no sun.
j To prevent wounds from becoming septic.
k To write notes or to leave as trail-markers.
l For first-aid (cuts, bites, etc.)
m To make a noise so as to attract attention.
n To light fires by catching the sun's rays or for signalling.
o For emergency water-containers or for signalling.
p To avoid catching common infectious diseases from dirty water.
q To light fires or a candle quickly.
r To be used as a reflector for a fire or a candle, or to make a cooking pot or drinking cup.

3.2 Now put these items in their order of importance. If you could only choose ten, which would you choose?

Reprinted by permission of Penguin Books Ltd.

4   Two days after it was sent, the bottle was found by three people on Kopia island. They knew Stewart Island fairly well, and considering the currents in the ocean, they assumed that the bottle must have come from the south of the island, somewhere around the place marked X on the map below. They decided that they would do all they could to try and rescue Peter Wrightson but first of all, they discussed his chances of survival. Of course, he must have sent the letter a few days before and he had probably – as he said – tried to explore the island during those two days. And they knew some parts of the island were very dangerous. Listen to their conversation.

4.1   Note down on the map your teacher will give you the dangers that can be found in different parts of the island.

4.2   Once you have completed the map, decide which route would be the safest for the rescuers to reach Peter Wrightson at point X.

5   You can now read a story that was published in *Life* magazine in 1972. The best way for you to read it is not to stop when you find a word you do not know; instead try to get the general meaning of the passage.
     When you have finished reading, try to answer the questions.

She lived and 91 others died

by Robert G Hummerstone

Haggard, bruised, still dazed, 17-year-old Juliane Koepcke gazed out of the light plane carrying her back to civilization from an incredible ordeal in the Peruvian wilds. Far below, scattered in the treetops and over the floor of the jungle, lay the bits and pieces of the airliner that Juliane had been riding in when it broke apart in mid-air and crashed. And hidden in the jungle were the broken bodies of her 91 fellow passengers. Almost miraculously, Juliane had been spared. Somehow, this delicate, almost frail-looking girl had not only survived the long fall from the plane, but had managed, for nine days, to stay alive in the wilderness.

Juliane's odyssey started with joyful anticipation. She had just graduated from high school in Lima, the capital, and now was going home for Christmas to her parents' remote home in the jungle. About 5'5" and weighing barely 100 pounds, she was the only child of two German-born scientists: animal ecologist Hans Koepcke and his ornithologist wife, Marie.

Juliane, her mother and a cheerful Christmas Eve crowd boarded the Lockheed Electra for the hour-and-a-half flight to the jungle town of Pucallpa. The plane climbed over the towering grey Andes and began its long descent into the flat, green Amazon valley below. There was no sign of trouble when the pilot instructed the passengers to fasten their seat-belts for the landing at Pucallpa.

Suddenly, the Electra was sledge-hammered by a violent jungle storm. Juliane saw a searing, lightning-like flash. Flames tore over the right wing. Alarmed, she looked at her mother, who said: 'This is the end of everything.' That was the last Juliane saw of her.

The next moment, Juliane felt as if she was being blown through the air. Strapped in her seat, she felt herself twisting, whirling, falling.

Juliane first heard the jungle birds. A canopy of green trees screened the late afternoon sunlight from above. About three hours had passed. She was lying on the jungle floor, still in her airplane seat. The two seats next to her were empty. There seemed to be no other people around. She called, but no one answered. There was a pain in her right shoulder – her collar-bone was fractured – and a cut on her upper right arm. Besides these and some bruises and scratches, she seemed otherwise unhurt.

Though probably suffering from shock, she never lost her wits or the confidence that she would be found. She had spent much of her childhood in the jungle with her parents and she remembered that her father had taught her to walk downhill to find water and then to follow the water downstream. Eventually, he had said, as the stream becomes bigger, one is bound to find civilization.

She began pushing through the thick underbrush. The rain had turned the ground into a muddy swamp and her high-heeled shoes sank in. The underbrush ripped at her dress. After a while, she lost one shoe and stumbled on for a day with one bare foot. Then she lost the other.

During the first three days after the crash, Juliane heard planes and helicopters searching above her for survivors, but they could not see her through the dense growth of jungle trees.

On Sunday, two days after the crash, she reached a narrow *quebrada*, or riverbed, at the headwaters of the Sheboya River and began to follow it. In many places she found it easier to swim along with the current than to walk. Her bare feet became black and blue; in some areas the ground was covered with thorns.

After the first three days, rain fell continually, and she was always wet. At night, shivering under trees, she slept only intermittently. She tried unsuccessfully to start a fire with her watch crystal. Insects and leeches bit her and her bites and cuts became infested with wormy larvae laid by flies. She saw few wild animals; some small crocodiles slithered off the shore after her in curiosity.

She ate nothing. She considered trying to catch some frogs, but was not sure which ones were poisonous. She picked some fruit and licked it hungrily but, again, she dared not eat it lest it be poisonous.

Four days after the crash, Juliane reached a small, thatched lean-to on the bank of the river. She had covered about ten air miles, but far more along her winding river course. Too weak to go any farther, she dragged herself inside and found some kerosene and salt.

After five days in the lean-to – nine days after the plane crashed – three hunters came by in a canoe. Struggling to the river bank, she waved and attracted their attention. The superstitious jungle men drew back, certain that the blond girl was some sort of evil spirit, but eventually they came ashore and gave her sugar, salt and some *fariña* meal. With gasoline, they helped her clean more worms out of her skin.

The next morning, two more hunters appeared and took Juliane in their canoe to the hut of a native woman for further help. When the woman saw the red of Juliane's bloodshot eyes, she screamed 'Demon!' and tried to chase them away.

The hunters then took Juliane to the small settlement of Tournavista. There, a doctor treated her cuts and bruises and bandaged her. The following day, 11 days after the crash, an American woman pilot, Jerrie Cobb, flew into the jungle airstrip and took Juliane to a camp of American missionaries at Yarinacocha, near Pucallpa, where she was reunited with her father.

5.1 Choose the best answer. You may refer to the text.

a The other passengers on the plane were
- [ ] hurt.
- [ ] killed.
- [ ] rescued later.

b Juliane was going
- [ ] home from Lima.
- [ ] to Lima.
- [ ] back to high school.

c Juliane's parents
- [ ] worked in the jungle.
- [ ] had gone to the jungle for Christmas.
- [ ] lived in Germany.

d Juliane's plane caught fire
- [ ] for some unknown reason.
- [ ] because of engine trouble.
- [ ] because it was struck by lightning.

e Juliane did not panic because
- [ ] she was in a state of shock.
- [ ] she knew civilization was not very far away.
- [ ] she was used to the jungle and knew what to do.

f Juliane followed a river because
- [ ] it was easier as she could swim instead of walk.
- [ ] she thought it would lead her to civilization.
- [ ] there were no trees above and she could be seen by the planes looking for her.

g Juliane did not eat anything because
- [ ] there was nothing to eat.
- [ ] she did not like what she found.
- [ ] she was afraid what she found would not be good for her.

h Juliane
- [ ] spent one night in a hut, then went on down the river.
- [ ] stopped walking after she reached the hut.
- [ ] reached a hut where she found some hunters.

i The hunters
   ☐ helped Juliane at once.
   ☐ helped Juliane only because she had blond hair.
   ☐ helped Juliane although they were suspicious at first.

j ☐ The hunters took Juliane to her father.
   ☐ Some missionaries came to fetch Juliane in the jungle.
   ☐ Juliane was carried by plane to a missionary camp.

5.2 How well can you guess the meaning of the words you do not know?

Work with a partner and try to answer the following questions. You can probably guess by simply looking at the sentence in which a word appears.

Paragraph 1 (Haggard …)
The three words used to describe Juliane (*haggard*, *bruised*, *dazed*) suggest
☐ happiness.
☐ shock.
☐ surprise.

In the paragraph, find synonyms for:
• a difficult time.
• an aeroplane.
• to be saved.
• the jungle.

Below (line 4) means ☐ above.
                    ☐ near.
                    ☐ under.

Paragraph 3 (Juliane, her mother …)
Find the verbs corresponding to the drawings.

The passengers are … the plane.

The plane is going to … .

Paragraphs 4 and 5 (Suddenly … falling.)
Find at least five verbs of movement in this passage.

Paragraph 6 (Juliane first heard …)
screened (line 2) means ☐ showed.
                         ☐ reflected.
                         ☐ hid.
Find four words showing that Juliane is a little hurt.

Paragraph 7 (Though probably suffering …)
Find an expression meaning the same thing as 'to be sure to'.

Paragraph 8 (She began …)
A *swamp* is ☐ hard ground.
            ☐ grass.
            ☐ soft wet land.
To *stumble* means ☐ to run.
                  ☐ to walk with difficulty.
                  ☐ to walk quickly.

Paragraph 11 (After the first three days …)
You *shiver* when you are ☐ thirsty.
                         ☐ cold.
                         ☐ hot.

Paragraph 13 (Four days after the crash …)
Find a word which means 'to move with difficulty'. What would a 'winding river' look like? Draw a line to show this.

4
The blind shall see

Whose fault if I'm blind?

75% of the 17,500,000 blind people in developing countries would be able to see, if adequate help were available.

1   Read the following introduction very carefully. It contains quite a lot of information. Try to imagine the scene.

A Land Rover approaches the village. Clouds of dust follow it. It turns into the market square and halts under the big tree in the middle, its back turned towards the school. The eye-doctor has arrived.

Within an hour and a half the doctor, his assistant, and the driver have pitched a large tent between the Land Rover and the school and have unloaded all their equipment. The tent now looks like a small hospital and the smell of the hospital is there, too.

In the corner of the market square Joseph sits in the shade of one of the trees that shield the school from the sun. The driver has installed a small gas-cooker alongside the Land Rover. Joseph watches him while he cooks a meal: sweet potatoes and beans and meat from a tin. He knows him very well. James Kabaala comes from the village, which he left when he was only twelve. He went to Jinja and attended a good school. Then he was trained by Doctor Burkitt to take part in the work of the Mobile Eye Unit and, with the doctor and his assistant William Likimani, he now travels to all the villages of this district.

Miss Beti, Joseph's teacher, has told them all about the work of the Mobile Eye Unit. Tomorrow the doctor will examine the eyes of all the children. Quite a few of Joseph's friends suffer from eye disease and some fear they may go blind like Sitolé, who cannot go to school and play with the other children. Joseph wishes the doctor could make Sitolé see again, if only enough to recognize his father and mother and little sister.

Sitolé is a nice boy, and he plays the recorder so well. Often Joseph and his friends sit listening when he is playing the tunes he has heard his mother sing.

Oh, here's Miss Beti. She is talking to James, probably about tomorrow.

2   Now, without looking at the text again, find out how much you remember.
    Afterwards you can check your answers.

2.1 Here's the market square. Draw the various symbols for the objects and
    people mentioned in the right positions:

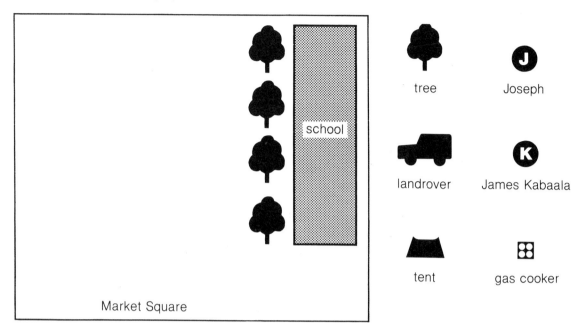

tree	Joseph
landrover	James Kabaala
tent	gas cooker

2.2

Burkitt	
Kabaala	
Likimani	
Joseph	
Beti	
Sitolé	
Sitolé's mother	
Joseph's friends	

What does the text say about these people? (Make
brief notes only.) You may look back at the text.
Check your notes with your partner.

2.3

personnel	
equipment	
destination	
duties	
meal	

What does it say about the Mobile Eye Unit? Check
with your partner again.

3   Read through the conversation below the chart between James Kabaala and
     Miss Beti. You will see that it may be divided into four parts. Can you find out
     where each part ends? In the second column of the chart some clues have
     been given which will help you to remember the dialogue. Complete this
     column. Do this with a partner. Afterwards try to create the dialogue with the
     help of the clues and act it out with your partner.

parts of the conversation	speakers and clues
a Miss Beti and James meet and talk about the arrangements for the next day.	Miss Beti — eye-clinic ready? James — early tomorrow/children at eight? Miss Beti — all/with father or mother/letter James — he'll need history
b They discuss eye-trouble with children …	James — many kids eye-trouble?
c … and possible ways to prevent this.	
d Then they talk about Sitolé.	

Miss Beti Ah, James. Good to see you again.
Everything ready in your eye-clinic?

James Oh yes, Miss Beti. We can start very early
tomorrow. Have you told the children to be
there at eight?

Miss Beti They will all be there. I've told them to
bring their father or mother, if possible, you
know … the doctor asked us in his letter.

James Oh yes, he'll need them … for the
case-history, you know. They can tell him a lot.
When was the first pain … or, whether there's
something in the family. Are there many kids
with eye-trouble?

Miss Beti Well, yes. Quite a few. It's the flies, you
see. Some of them don't wash their faces
much. I've told them about the daily face wash,
but …

James I know. You can't change their habits
easily.

Miss Beti No, and the flies, you know, and the dirty
fingers and rags … they carry the infection from
one eye to another … there isn't often very
much water.

James Couldn't you fix up a gutter on the school
roof and collect rainwater in a container?

Miss Beti Not a bad idea. I'll discuss it with the
parents … we could have a daily face wash
every morning … then perhaps they'll continue
it at home.

James Yes, the school can do a lot. It's so … so
important … the prevention of eye diseases …

once they're blind … there's not much you can do.

Miss Beti We … have one boy, such a nice boy. It would be marvellous if he could be cured. Perhaps an operation could help him. But his parents are very poor. Perhaps you know him? Sitolé.

James Oh yes … yes, I know his father. We were good friends when I was a boy … I'll ask the doctor. Perhaps we can find a way. But don't say anything. I can't promise the doctor can help him.

Miss Beti Thank you, James. It would be wonderful if he could.

4

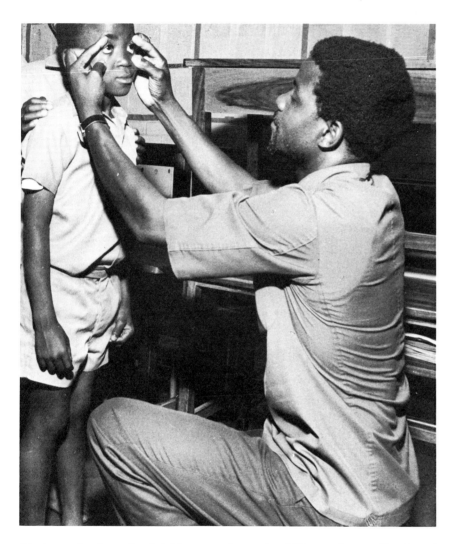

Next morning the school children are all examined. Those who need treatment are treated by the doctor, James, and the other assistant. First the doctor, Doctor Burkitt, asks a lot of questions and the parents try to answer them. Miss Beti translates their answers for the doctor, who then takes down brief notes. This is the form he uses. It was completed for Sitolé when Doctor Burkitt examined him for the first time.

What were the questions he asked? Write them out yourself first, then compare with your partner.

MOBILE EYE UNIT 1

Medical officer in charge: *Dr. Burkitt*

Assistant 1: *William Likimani*

Driver: *James Kabaala*

Visit to: *Iganga*

If visit to a school, name of school: *Primary School*

Date(s) of visit: *March 21st*

Name of patient: *Sitole*

Age: *eleven*

Profession: *not applicable*

(If child) profession of father: *farmer*

Main symptom:

pain	☐
loss of sight	☑
bad vision	☐
double vision	☐

Affected eye(s)　left ☑　　*probably developmental cataract*

　　　　　　　　right ☑

Symptom first noticed: *at age of 12 months*

Eye disease(s) in family: *uncle and cousin*

Patient suffers from other disease(s): *no*

If eye(s) have been injured in an accident:

What sort of accident? *not applicable*

5.1 In the second part of the following paragraph you can see what Doctor Burkitt actually said to Miss Beti. Try to write the first part of the paragraph as a conversation too.

Miss Beti herself was a little worried too. Especially after a day's teaching and a lot of studying at night, her eyes ached a little and she could not see properly. She thought she might need glasses. The doctor examined her carefully and then told her that her eyes were normal. Glasses would not help, except to make her look wiser! 'The trouble is', he told her, 'that the small muscles inside your eyes have to work much harder than normal because of the amount of reading you do. Perhaps you read, as many students do, by a poor light and also you hold the book much too close to your eyes. I shall give you some rules so that you can learn to help your eyes.'

5.2 Here are the rules he gave her:

1 Hold your book at least 60 cm away from your face and sit up straight when reading or writing at a desk.

2 Rest your eyes from time to time by looking away in the distance for a minute or so.

3 At night, use the brightest light you can, and if possible, sit so that the light shines over your left shoulder on to your paper or book.

4 When your eyes ache with too much reading, bathe them with cold water.

5 Most students believe that the more they read, the more they learn. This is a mistake, because when your eyes and brain become tired, you no longer understand properly what you are reading, and so your reading becomes a waste of time.

It is therefore better to read for a short time and understand what you read, than to read for a long time and yet absorb little or nothing.

Look at the following photographs. In some of them Esther is observing one of the rules given and therefore deserves praise. In some of them she has clearly forgotten a rule for which she must be corrected. Imagine you are with her in the room.

Write out completely one of the following sentences for each picture:

- If she deserves praise:
  'That's right. It is very sensible of you to ....'

- If you must correct her:
  'Esther, you had better not (should not) ....'
  'Why don't you .... ?'

a ....

b ....

c ....

d ....

e ....

f ....

6   Read the following text. Can you suggest a title?

After Doctor Burkitt had examined Sitolé once more, he decided that he would operate upon one eye now and, if the operation proved to be successful, he would operate upon the other eye after three or four months when he visited Iganga again. The operation was scheduled for the next morning. Sitolé and his father and mother were very happy, although Doctor Burkitt told them he could not promise success.

Early in the morning Doctor Burkitt, William, and James started the preparations. Sterile towels and dressings were unpacked from one of the cases, and the instruments were boiled. Then Sitolé was laid out on a table, his head under a spot-lamp, which was run off the car battery. His head and shoulders were covered with plastic towelling.

The operation itself did not take very long. A local anaesthetic was used. Doctor Burkitt was assisted by William and James, who, like him, wore caps, masks, and aprons. After the operation the eye was covered with a sterile dressing.

Doctor Burkitt was very pleased with the operation itself, but they would have to wait for a couple of days to see if it had been successful.

6.1   Use the text above to make a list about the preparations for the operation on Sitolé and the operation itself. Then use your notes to give an eye-witness report for the other members of your group.

6.2   A reporter from the Kenya Broadcasting Service happened to be in Iganga. He heard about Sitolé and made a telephone call to the editor in the main office in Nairobi. In the conversation below you will see only what the editor said on the Nairobi end of the line. Can you guess what the reporter's words were? Compare your ideas with your partner.

Reporter   ....
Editor   Hello? This is George Muindi. Who's speaking?
Reporter   ....
Editor   Yes, I've got it now. What do you want me to do?
Reporter   ....
Editor   Oh certainly. It would be interesting to say something about it in ... er ... Saturday's programme. Which ... er ... Unit is it? Any names?
Reporter   ....
Editor   I see. Now tell me about the boy. How often has this Doctor Burkitt seen him?
Reporter   ....
Editor   What has he decided?
Reporter   ....
Editor   What, both eyes?
Reporter   ....
Editor   Ah yes, of course. What about the parents?

Reporter   ....
Editor   And ... er ... what are the chances?
Reporter   ....
Editor   I see. Now, could you be there in the morning and give an eye-witness report?
Reporter   ....
Editor   Of course not. I forgot the Unit's got no telephone.
Reporter   ....
Editor   Marvellous. Now, after you've made the tape, send it off straightaway.
Reporter   ....
Editor   Sure, I'll call you when we have it. Thanks for calling me.
Reporter   ....
Editor   Goodbye.

When you have finished, check your ideas with the recording.

6.3 Six months later the following article appeared in the *Kenya Times*:

NEW SUCCESS FOR MOBILE EYE UNIT

In this paper we have often reported on the important work done by the Mobile Eye Units throughout East Africa. Last week a spectacular success was scored in Iganga, where Dr Burkitt's Unit performed a second operation on young Sitolé (11), who had not been able to see since the age of one.

Bright student

Said his teacher, Miss Beti (26): 'We are so happy for Sitolé. He's a bright kid and all the children love him. I expect he will be able to go to a secondary school now that he is no longer handicapped.'

Glasses

'Of course, he will have to wear glasses', William Likimani, one of the team who carried out the operation told us. 'But, that's no problem. It will make him look even smarter.'

7 Choose one of the following assignments:

a You have now heard of the existence of the Mobile Eye Units and their work in East Africa. You have decided to try and collect some money for them with a group of friends. Decide on what you are going to do and why, and write this in a letter to the *Kenya Times* in Nairobi.

b Write a poem together!
Every member of your group writes one line completing the sentence 'When you cannot see …', and one line completing the sentence 'But if you can see …'. Then collect all the lines and decide on the order in which you'll put them together to form a poem.

c Prepare a poster to make the work of the Mobile Eye Unit better known, and asking for funds to support it.

Postscript

The story of this chapter is not completely authentic, but based on reality: on the work of many institutions and foundations working in developing countries (for example, the Busoga Eye Project in Uganda) and on the experience of specialists who travel and work in those countries.

Details about the work of the Mobile Eye Units have been taken from A Handbook of Ophthalmology for Developing Countries, Geoffrey G. Bisley, O.U.P. 1973.

5

The mystery of the Simplon Express

1 The facts

Read the following information and try to solve the mystery based on a short story by Agatha Christie.

On May 2nd, Mrs Elsie Jeffries discovered the loss of all her jewels as she was travelling on the Simplon Express. The jewels, worth £41,000, were kept in a small case which Mrs Jeffries carried everywhere with her.

Mrs Elsie Jeffries
A young American
woman

The sleeping-car

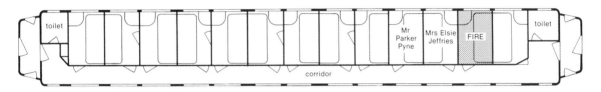

Mr Parker Pyne
A private detective

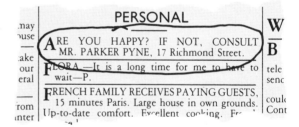

1.1 Mrs Jeffries

As soon as the train starts, Mrs Elsie Jeffries decides to tell Mr Parker Pyne about her worries: listen to their conversation and make notes about what you learn.

Elsie's situation in life.	
Where she's going.	
What worries her.	

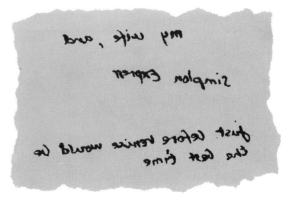

What Elsie found on the blotter.

2 The journey

Here is what happened just before the train reached Venice:

Suddenly a scream broke out from the corridor.

'Oh, look – look! The train is on fire!'

With a bound Elsie and Mr Parker Pyne were in the corridor. An agitated woman with a Slav countenance was pointing a dramatic finger. Out of one of the front compartments smoke was pouring in a cloud. Mr Parker Pyne and Elsie ran along the corridor. Others joined them. The compartment in question was full of smoke. The first comers drew back, coughing. The conductor appeared.

'The compartment is empty!' he cried. 'Do not alarm yourselves, *messieurs et dames. Le feu*, it will be controlled.'

A dozen excited questions and answers broke out. The train was running over the bridge that joins Venice to the mainland.

Suddenly Mr Parker Pyne turned, forced his way through the little pack of people behind him and hurried down the corridor to Elsie's compartment. The lady with the Slav face was seated in it, drawing deep breaths from the open window.

'Excuse me, Madame,' said Parker Pyne. 'But this is not your compartment.'

'I know. I know,' said the Slav lady, '*Pardon*. It is the shock, the emotion – my heart.' She sank back on the seat and indicated the open window. She drew her breath in great gasps.

Mr Parker Pyne stood in the doorway. His voice was fatherly and reassuring. 'You must not be afraid,' he said, 'I do not think for a moment that the fire is serious.'

'Not? Ah, what a mercy! I feel restored.' She half-rose. 'I will return to my own compartment.'

'Not just yet,' Mr Parker Pyne's hand pressed her gently back. 'I will ask you to wait a moment, Madame.'

'Monsieur, this is an outrage!'

'Madame, you will remain.'

His voice rang out coldly. The woman sat still looking at him. Elsie joined them.

'It seems it was a smoke bomb,' she said breathlessly. 'Some ridiculous practical joke. The conductor is furious. He is asking everybody —' She broke off, staring at the second occupant of the carriage.

'Mrs Jeffries,' said Mr Parker Pyne, 'what do you carry in your little scarlet case?'

'My jewellery.'

'Perhaps you would be so kind as to look and see that everything is there.'

There was immediately a torrent of words from the Slav lady. She broke into French, the better to do justice to her feelings.

In the meantime Elsie had picked up the jewel case. 'Oh!' she cried. 'It's unlocked.'

'*... Et je porterai plainte à la Compagnie des Wagons-Lits,*' finished the Slav lady.

'They're gone!' cried Elsie. 'Everything! My diamond bracelet. And the necklace Pop gave me. And the emerald and ruby rings. And some lovely diamond brooches. Thank goodness I was wearing my pearls. Oh, Mr Pyne, what shall we do?'

'If you fetch the conductor,' said Mr Parker Pyne, 'I will see that this woman does not leave this compartment till he comes.'

'*Scélérat! Monstre!*' shrieked the Slav lady. She went on to further insults. The train drew in to Venice.

The events of the next half-hour may be briefly summarized. Mr Parker Pyne dealt with several different officials in several different languages – and suffered defeat. The suspected lady consented to be searched – and emerged without a stain on her character. The jewels were not on her.

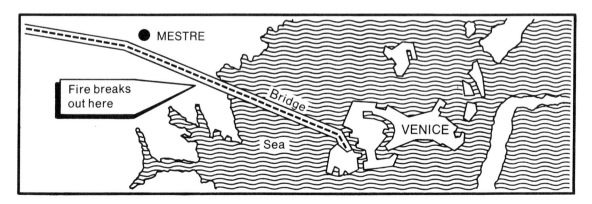

Elsie and Parker Pyne later search Elsie Jeffries' compartment again; but the jewels are not there.

2.1 On the right, you will find a list of all the events in the text. Can you put them in their correct order?

- Scream in the corridor.
- Elsie realizes her jewels have been stolen.
- The train arrives in Venice.
- The conductor reassures everybody.
- People run into the corridor.
- Parker Pyne and Elsie leave the compartment.
- Parker Pyne reassures the Slav lady.
- A woman shows them where the fire is.
- The man in charge of the train arrives.
- The Slav lady is searched.
- Parker Pyne goes back to Elsie's compartment.
- The train crosses the bridge.
- The Slav lady wants to return to her compartment.
- The jewels are not found on the Slav lady.
- The Slav lady decides she will complain about Parker Pyne's behaviour.
- The Slav lady is recovering near the window.

2.2 Work in pairs. Tell the story of the fire in your own words. You can use the list of events on the right to help you. Use the following adverbs to link your story together:

First ...
Then ...
At that moment ...
At once ...
A short time later ...
While .../As ...
Meanwhile ...
Still/Not yet

2.3 Certain events in the story are mentioned in these two columns. Using one of the following adverbs, make sentences combining two of these events (one from the left-hand column and one from the right-hand column): *when/before/after/while/as/just as.*

For example: *After arriving in Venice, the Slav lady agreed to be searched.*

- scream
- Parker Pyne and Elsie reach the compartment that is on fire
- the fire breaks out
- Parker Pyne goes back to Elsie's compartment
- people ask the conductor questions
- Elsie opens her jewel-case
- arrival in Venice

- the Slav lady is searched
- train over the bridge to Venice
- Elsie's diamonds have disappeared
- the conductor arrives
- Parker Pyne and Elsie rush into the corridor
- Slav lady in Elsie's compartment

3 A few clues

The following facts will perhaps help you to solve the mystery:

- Only two people have a key to Elsie's jewel-case: her husband and herself.
- Mr Jeffries has financial difficulties.
- The Slav lady, Mrs Subaysha, knows Elsie's husband. She is also a great admirer of diamonds and once saw Elsie's at a party.
- Elsie's husband is fundamentally honest and loves his wife.
- Parker Pyne sent a telegram from the next station (Trieste) and that allowed him to recover the jewels in Constantinople when he arrived there.

4   **Who did it?**

Now, find out what happened.

With a partner try to answer the questions in the table your teacher will give you. If you are still uncertain, you can write down two possibilities each time (A and B) and note the arguments for and against each one. Then put a circle round those you finally choose. Be prepared to explain your choices in the class discussion.

5

Work in pairs to discuss this picture.

a What exactly has happened?

b Who are those two people? Do they know each other? What do they do in life? Would you say the woman (a) is a professional thief? (b) just badly needs money at the moment? (c) does it for fun?

c Imagine the man turns round and sees the woman. What would he say to her? Would she try to justify herself? How?

d The man decides to call the guard. Imagine the scene and the conversation that would follow.

e Play the scene as if you and your partner were the people in the picture. (You may make notes first if you wish.)

f Now listen to the conversations on the tape.

6 Now read the following text on Agatha Christie.

Writer, Top selling

The all-time estimate of book sales by Erle Stanley Gardner (1889–1970) (US) to 1 Jan 1980 was 311,803,986 copies in 37 languages. The top-selling authoress has been Dame Agatha Christie (née Miller) (later Lady Mallowan) (1890–1976) whose 87 crime novels sold an estimated 300,000,000 in 103 languages. *Sleeping Murder* was published posthumously in 1977.

In such words does the *Guinness Book of World Records* describe the Mistress of Mystery, Agatha Christie. Her books include detective stories (many of which have been made into films), short stories, romances and plays (one of which, *The Mousetrap*, is now the world's longest-running play with well over 10,000 performances!) As for her earnings, they are estimated at well over $20 million.

Who was Dame Agatha Christie? Her father was a rich American financier, but she grew up in the English countryside, among the genteel upper middle-class society she describes so well in her books. During the First World War, she married Colonel Christie and served as a nurse. From her experience in hospitals at the time, she developed an interest in poisons which was to be so useful to her later in many of her stories. She divorced her husband in 1928 and a few years later, married Sir Max Mallowan, a young archaeologist. She accompanied him on many of his expeditions and drew from them the plot of several of her novels.

Agatha Christie started writing just after World War I, as a kind of challenge. She had no success with her first book, which no publisher wanted to take and which did not sell very well. It was only with the publication of *The Murder of Roger Ackroyd* in 1926 that she suddenly became well-known. From then on, her books followed each other regularly. Her two favourite detectives were Hercule Poirot, the small Belgian with his long moustache, his egg-shaped head and his quick brain, and Miss Marple, the shrewd old-fashioned lady who solves all problems by making comparisons with the people she knows in her small village. For Miss Marple, just as for Agatha Christie, human nature is the same everywhere, and good and evil are at work in all social classes, amongst all nations.

Where did she get her ideas from? Mostly from the people around her, people she knew or had read about. In the introduction to one of her books, Agatha Christie wrote:

'… you don't invent your settings. They are outside you, all around you, in existence – you have only to stretch out your hand and pick and choose. A railway train, a hospital, a London hotel, a Caribbean beach, a country village, a cocktail party, a girls' school.

But only one thing matters – they must be there – in existence. Real people, real places. A definite place in time and space. If here and now – how shall you get full information – apart from the evidence of your own eyes and ears? The answer is frighteningly simple.

It is what the Press brings to you every day, served up in your morning paper under the general heading of News. Collect it from the front page.'

But usually, the ideas for her plots came to her while she was doing housework: cooking, washing, working in the garden. She even said that much of her inspiration came whilst eating apples in a hot bath!

In spite of her amazing success, Agatha Christie remained extremely modest. She once said: 'Nothing has surprised me more than to have become a famous authoress.'

6.1 Here are several statements about Agatha Christie. Decide whether they
     are true or false, and correct them if you think they are false.

		true	false
1	Agatha Christie always expected she would become famous.	☐	☐
2	Because she had always been interested in chemistry, Agatha Christie chose to work in a hospital during the war.	☐	☐
3	Agatha Christie said she got most of her ideas from reading the newspapers.	☐	☐
4	Agatha Christie did not write only detective stories.	☐	☐
5	All of Agatha Christie's stories are set in places she knew well in England.	☐	☐
6	For Miss Marple the solution to most mysteries lies in the study of human nature.	☐	☐
7	Agatha Christie became famous immediately after the publication of her first novel.	☐	☐
8	Agatha Christie believed in the existence of good and evil.	☐	☐

6.2 Here is what an encyclopedia says about Agatha Christie. Can you complete
     the entry?

CHRISTIE, Agatha, Mary, Clarissa, Miller
English .... (born ...., died ....). After
........., she became famous with .... She
wrote .... novels. Some of her creations such
as .... have become famous characters of English fiction. In 1928, she .... Later she married .... and often .... on his travels
abroad. Many of her ideas for plots came to her
as she ....

6

Did you have a good holiday?

1   Most of us dream of the coming summer holidays. But did you know the way you spend your holidays can tell a lot about your character? If you want to know more about yourself, try answering these questions as truthfully as possible.

A   Where would you prefer to spend your holidays?
1 in the country
2 at the seaside
3 in the mountains
4 in a far-away, exotic country

B   Which of these four landscapes most appeals to you?
1 a little fishing village with white-washed houses and green hills behind
2 a beautiful mountain lake with dark forests around and mist in the air
3 the view from a mountain top on a clear day, when you can see for miles
4 a large garden with trees and a lot of flowers

C   Who would you prefer to go with?
1 just with your best friend
2 with a group of friends
3 on your own
4 with your family

D   What would you most hate?
1 missing your plane/boat and having to change some of your plans
2 having rain all the time and not being able to admire the landscape you came for
3 having to take some urgent work that you must do during your holiday
4 staying in a very noisy hotel

E   How would you most enjoy spending one of your days?
1 going on a picnic with friends you have made at the hotel or camp-site
2 sunbathing on the beach or in the garden
3 going for a long walk that you have planned beforehand
4 spending the day out on a boat

F   You've been out in the mountains for the day with two friends and you get lost. Night falls and you have to sleep in a small hut. Would you
1 love it because it's a real adventure?
2 worry about what you will do in the morning?
3 think it will be all right in the morning?
4 try to make everybody comfortable for the night?

G   How would you prefer to have your meals during the holidays?
1 buying food from local shops and cooking your own meals
2 taking all the meals in the hotel where you're staying
3 eating in different places every day – wherever you are
4 going to typical local restaurants

H   When you are travelling by train, what do you usually choose to do?
1 look out of the window and day-dream
2 think of what you will do when you arrive
3 read books and magazines
4 try to talk with the people sitting next to you

What's your score?

A 1 = c 2 = d 3 = b 4 = a
B 1 = c 2 = a 3 = b 4 = d
C 1 = a 2 = d 3 = b 4 = c
D 1 = b 2 = a 3 = d 4 = c
E 1 = d 2 = c 3 = b 4 = a
F 1 = a 2 = b 3 = d 4 = c
G 1 = b 2 = c 3 = d 4 = a
H 1 = a 2 = b 3 = c 4 = d

Add up the number of times you score a, b, c or d.

Now work with a partner and see what kind of person he/she is. Use these notes to help you. Do you both agree with the interpretation of your character?

If you get mainly a, then you are romantic and imaginative. You like romance and mystery and feel very strongly and intensely about everything that happens to you.

If you get mainly b, you are a practical person. You are serious and you like working, but you prefer doing things and planning new projects. You enjoy organizing things.

If you get mainly c, it means you are a quiet, serious and sensible person. You like regular habits and you're fond of thinking and reading. You are mainly a 'family person'.

If you get mainly d, you're a relaxed and happy person! You don't worry much about anything and you like having people around you all the time.

2 Susan

Now look at these answers given by Susan:
A = 2   B = 2   C = 2   D = 3   E = 1
F = 1   G = 4   H = 4

How do you interpret her character?

Susan is twenty-six. She works in an advertising agency in London. She doesn't get very long holidays, but this year she has decided to travel. She'd like to go somewhere where she can swim and make a lot of friends. In fact, she is still hesitating between three possibilities. Here they are:

GREEK VILLAGE
TWO WEEKS FROM £119

You know you'll enjoy Greek Village because it comes from those wonderful folk who brought you Camp Africa.

On the unspoilt island of Thassos, people between 18 and 30 get together to enjoy a holiday — your way.

Do what you want, when you want. No grannies or kids are going to get in your way. There's water skiing, windsurfing, expeditions, discos, beach barbeques, Greek dancing, parties — or just laze on the beach all day.

Do everything. Do nothing. The choice is yours. Two weeks to remember for as little as £119.

For more details about Greek Village — or Camp Africa in Morocco — phone or post the coupon for a free brochure.

Young World Holidays, P.O. Box 99,
29 Queens Road, Brighton BN1 3YN
Tel: 0273-23397

Name _____

Address _____

_____

_____

Postcode _____
ATOL 782B

DO YOU DREAM OF . . .

Fascinating scenery? Moonlight drinks on the deck? Picturesque villages?

Then come on a cruise with **Xenophon Tours.**

A LEISURELY CRUISE ● Luxurious air-conditioned ship ● Spacious cabins with private toilet ● Swimming-pool on large deck ● Chaises-longues for everybody ● First-class food and excellent service.

A UNIQUE EXPERIENCE Discover the coast of Greece and the delights of the Aegean Islands. For people who love romantic and majestic scenery. Freedom to explore these unspoilt islands on your own.

Prices from £280 for 7 days. For more details write to Xenophon Tours, 49 Gatwick Road, London SW8.

Guernsey
the charming
channel isle

Nestling in the Bay of St. Malo, so near and yet a world away from present day stresses, this beautiful holiday island offers you peace and relaxation in a unique atmosphere.

Excellent accommodation, restaurants, shops (no VAT), perfect bathing, plenty of entertainment, visits to the nearby islands of Alderney, Herm and Sark.

If you want to combine the pleasures of the seaside with quiet walks in the country, come to Guernsey with your family!

There's much more to tell you so please send for your FREE copy of our 240 page colour brochure by completing the coupon and posting it to: Guernsey Tourist Board Dept. 43A, P.O. Box 23, Guernsey, Channel Islands, or 'phone 0481 23557 (24hr, brochafone service).

Did you have a good holiday?   45

2.1 First read these advertisements. If you had to
decide where to go, which holiday would most
appeal to you? Why? Choose a partner and
discuss it with him/her.

Use the expressions you have already seen to
show your preference. If you don't agree with your
partner, the following starters may be useful:

(Yes) but …
On the other hand …
But if you …
I don't see why …

2.2 Read these advertisements again carefully. This time, list all the words and
expressions you can find to describe the following points:

	Guernsey	Greek Village	Xenophon Tours
comfort			
scenery			
peace and quiet			
romantic holiday			
entertainment			

2.3 There were four types of people mentioned in the quiz. Particular words are
used in the advertisements to attract particular types of people. For example,
'company' and 'parties' are mentioned to attract people who like to have
friends around them (mainly those people who got ds in the quiz). Make a list
of the words used to appeal to each type.

2.4 You know how Susan answered the quiz, so which holiday do you consider
best suited to her personality? Discuss your opinion with your partner.

3 Soon after Susan has arranged everything, she phones her friend Jim to tell
him what her plans are. Listen to their conversation and decide:

3.1 Which of the three possible holidays Susan has finally chosen.

3.2 The route she will follow. (Your teacher will give you an outline map.)

3.3 What plans she has made so far. Complete a form like this with your partner.

day	place	plans
Monday July 6th		
Tuesday		
Wednesday		
Thursday		
Friday		
Saturday		
Sunday		
Monday		

Dear Jim,

I can hardly believe we been here for nearly a week. I am getting so lazy that I haven't written to anybody yet, and I can remember promising myself I'd send postcards to everybody. Greece is too beautiful for words. I hadn't imagined it so wild and mountainous, and you keep discovering tiny villages and monasteries high up in the mountains. But unfortunately, the organization is terrible! For one thing, there are always changes in their plans. We stayed two days in Karistos (in the south of Evia) because they said there were some problems with the boat. And now they say they may not go to Skopelos after all as we're rather short of time – not that we stay anywhere for very long. The ship is always late and when we stop anywhere, we never have enough time to look round the island!

The ship is large and nice but the service is simply dreadful! The meals are awful and always the same! I seem to have been eating tomatoes 3 times a day since I arrived: When I think I was looking forward to having Greek food!

And the deck is always crowded so that I usually prefer sitting inside when we're on the boat. I've made quite a number of very nice friends and we have a lot of fun talking and relaxing. The trouble is that the air-conditioning stopped working yesterday and it's just unbearable inside now.

The whole thing is so badly run that it's hard to believe. You remember that advertisement I showed you? How could they possibly write all that? The only thing that was all right was the flight to Athens and _they_ probably don't organize that! I'm certainly going to ask for some of my money back when the tour is over!

Thank goodness there's the landscape and I've met a lot of lovely people so I'll be sorry when we get back to Athens in a couple of days. I'll ring you when I get home.

All my love,
Susan

4.1 As you can see from Susan's letter, some things which were promised by the advertisement were changed. Complete a table like this, listing the things which were true, and those which were different.

	as described in the advertisement	different from the advertisement
ship		
food		
atmosphere		
route		

4.2 What do you think she wrote on this comments card at the end of her tour?

```
┌─────────────────────────────────────────────┐
│ XENOPHON TOURS    COMMENTS CARD              │
└─────────────────────────────────────────────┘
```

We hope you enjoyed your holiday with us. As our first concern is your satisfaction, we would very much appreciate your comments. They will help us to maintain the standard of our tours.

D: dissatisfied
S: satisfied
VS: very satisfied

	D	S	VS	FURTHER COMMENTS
Flight				
Boat: cabin				
service				
meals				
entertainment				
Programme				

What made you choose Xenophon Tours? ....

....

Your suggestions: ....

....

....

5   As soon as she was back in London, Susan phoned Xenophon Tours to
     complain about the cruise and try to get some of her money back. Below
     you can read what Susan said in this conversation. Can you guess what
     the man answered on the other end of the line? Compare your answers
     with your partner.

Agent ....
Susan Hello. Is that Xenophon Tours?
Agent ....
Susan Good morning. My name is Susan Forbes
       and I'm just back from a cruise to Greece which
       I took with your organization.
Agent ....
Susan That's it. The group that came back
       yesterday.
Agent ....
Susan Well, not really, and this is the reason I'm
       phoning you. You see, everything seemed to be
       wrong from the very beginning.
Agent ....
Susan I'm certainly not exaggerating. Take the
       boat, for instance. According to your
       advertisement, everything should have been
       first-class. But the service was slow, and
       everyone agreed that the food was very poor ...
Agent ....
Susan That's no reason. I suppose most people
       don't take the trouble once the holiday is over.
       But I think it's unfair to ...

Agent ....
Susan But it wasn't only the meals! Everything
       was along that line. We didn't see Skopelos
       because we'd stayed too long somewhere else.
Agent ....
Susan I know. These things can happen, I
       suppose. But I don't see why we'd have to pay
       for things we didn't see. We all think you should
       refund some of the money we paid.
Agent ....
Susan But...but, surely
Agent ....
Susan But surely, if you promise something on
       your brochure, we have a right to see it!
Agent ....
Susan Look, I don't remember whether your
       contract mentioned it or not, but I'm certainly
       going to make sure that everyone knows about
       this. Goodbye!

Read again what Susan said and note all the expressions which she used to
complain or to express her dissatisfaction.
Now listen to the tape of the conversation and see if you guessed right.

6.1   Work with a partner. One of you will be Susan and will decide to phone the
      Consumers' Association to tell them about the holiday. Write the notes you
      would make before phoning, to remind you of what you have to say.

      The other will be a member of the staff of the Consumers' Association. Prepare
      a list of questions you usually ask people who phone with complaints, for
      example:

      Are you sure that ...?
      Have you got a copy of the advertisement?

      Finally, listen to the conversation as it really took place.

6.2   Use the above information and write the letter which Susan might send to the
      editor of her local paper.

7 You have been warned!

Now you know you should be careful when choosing your next holiday. The words on the travel brochure can mean something quite different from what you expect. For instance, the following words, 'breathtaking view of the bay' might refer to something like this:

So you had better think twice before you make up your mind. Imagine a friend of yours came to see you and was hesitating between the following possibilities. What would you tell him or her?

JUST THINK OF . . .

Those sun-drenched beaches in Italy; sampling local delicacies; staying in tiny and intimate alberghi; being free to explore as you choose. Holiday prices start from £150.

CAREFREE HOLIDAYS

Telephone us at 01-785 3619

To hire your own traditional cottage contact us at

HOLIDAY COTTAGES

We offer you a few days away from it all in one of our picturesque cottages in the South of England, East Anglia or Wales. Contact us at Norwich 60001.

Exotic Travel Ltd.

offers 14 festive nights in Hong Kong for £600. Enjoy the holiday of a lifetime, a unique experience — come to Hong Kong for Christmas! All the mystery of the Orient — a chance to visit the duty-free bargain bazaars, and see a different world.

For further information telephone:
Exotic Travel Limited: 01-794 2508 (24 hour reply service).

7.1 In the left-hand column below you will find some of the statements from the advertisements. Match them with a statement from the right-hand column, which might give a more realistic assessment.

Advertiser's claim
- sun-drenched beaches
- picturesque cottages
- 14 festive nights
- away from it all
- tiny and intimate
- local delicacies
- duty-free, bargain bazaars
- all the mystery of the Orient
- prices start from £150

Possible interpretation
- two weeks without sleep
- rooms so small you can't stand up straight
- uneatable food
- it will cost you a lot more than £150
- the noise and discomfort of the Far East
- beaches where it is too hot to stay in the sun for more than ten minutes
- uncomfortable old buildings in need of repair
- street markets where you will be encouraged to buy things you don't need
- bleak, lonely and difficult to find

8 Read the following article on travel agencies. While you are reading, try to concentrate on the following points.

- What is the problem?
- What evidence is given?
- What would be a solution to the problem?

When you have finished, discuss your ideas with a partner. Then check together on the meaning of any words or idioms you do not understand.

The Times, 14 September

When your travel agent gets it wrong

By Robin Young
Consumer Affairs
Correspondent

Travel agents frequently give outrageously bad advice or absolutely wrong information, the magazine *Holiday Which?* alleges today after anonymously inviting 115 agents to tackle holiday difficulties.

One agent, asked to recommend a hotel on Corfu took out an option on a holiday at a hotel on the island of Kos, 500 miles away. Others, asked for advice about the Bahamas, quoted a fare 'direct to Barbados', or recommended the island of St Lucia. Both Barbados and St Lucia are in the West Indies.

Asked for advice about crossing the Adriatic from Italy to Corfu, two agents said it was impossible and two others said the best way would be to drive all the way round to the Greek mainland and get a ferry from there. Another agent suggested taking a ferry from Naples to Piraeus, in Greece. In fact several companies operate ferry services from Brindisi to Corfu.

Even agents who did give the correct route were uncertain how frequently ferries ran, estimates varying from once a day to five times a day.

Most agents, the magazine says, seemed to start from the assumption that a package holiday would be cheaper than travelling independently. Few made any precise calculations to check that statement.

Five agents incorrectly said visas would be required for the Bahamas, and one inaccurately stated that a smallpox vaccination was necessary. Several did not know what the local currency was.

Holiday Which? concludes that it is clearly worth using a good agent to get the benefit of expert advice, but that good agents were thin on the ground. 'We were appalled by the results of our tests.'

Agents do not have to carry enormous stores of knowledge in their heads, the magazine says. The main thing they should know is where to look in their reference material to answer questions. 'We got some very reasonable service from inexperienced school-leavers who did make good use of the material', but agents 'could easily improve their service substantially'.

7
The National Health Service

1 The National Health Service in the United Kingdom.

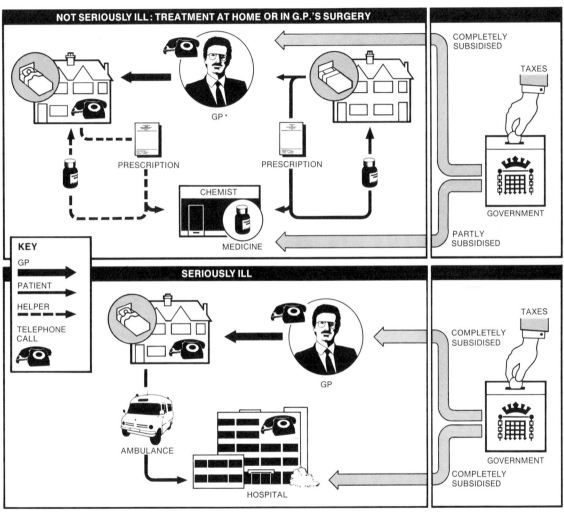

NOT SERIOUSLY ILL: TREATMENT AT HOME OR IN G.P.'S SURGERY

GP *

PRESCRIPTION

PRESCRIPTION

CHEMIST

MEDICINE

COMPLETELY SUBSIDISED

TAXES

GOVERNMENT

PARTLY SUBSIDISED

KEY

GP

PATIENT

HELPER

TELEPHONE CALL

SERIOUSLY ILL

GP

AMBULANCE

HOSPITAL

TAXES

COMPLETELY SUBSIDISED

GOVERNMENT

COMPLETELY SUBSIDISED

* G.P. = General Practitioner (family doctor)

1.1 What does a British citizen do when he or she is ill?

Look at the pictorial diagram above. What is the most important thing about the National Health Service in Great Britain?

1.2 Discuss very briefly what is done when someone in a British family has caught the measles or suffers from appendicitis? What happens in your country? Who pays?

2 The following part of a letter written by a foreigner to friends in Leeds may
   illustrate how organized and effective the system is.

Amsterdam
1st September

Dear Tony and Bernadette,

It was a pity we missed you by half a day! When we called at your house unexpectedly you had just gone off to Spain. Your neighbour told us he had seen you leave early in the morning. Of course we should have phoned, but we didn't know we were going to stay in your part of the country that long, as we had planned to go to Scotland straight away.

However, our little daughter Birgit fell off a slide while we were staying in the Municipal Camping site at Ripon. What followed was quite an experience, and we can assure you that you have every reason to be proud of your National Health Service! Birgit was unconscious for a few minutes and felt rather sick. She vomited and we both thought she might have concussion. Friends rang the local G.P. and within ten minutes he called at our caravan and examined her. He thought we had better take her to the hospital for a check-up and wanted to send for a ambulance, which would take her there, free! Well, I decided I could easily take her there in my car, which he did not object to, although he repeated his offer to call an ambulance.

Immediately after our arrival in Harrogate District Hospital Birgit was attended to, X-ray photographs were taken that showed nothing had been broken, and she was put to bed. A room was offered for one of the parents to stay with her! Again we felt a little uneasy. We didn't want to be a nuisance and I said I could easily come back during the night to see how she was. When I came back I discovered she was happily asleep. An extremely friendly male nurse told me they were worried that Birgit did not speak English, and they might not be able to communicate with her. Fortunately Sister Alice, who would be on duty next day, spoke some French. He was a little disappointed when I told him that Birgit, like so many continentals, did not speak French either. Anyway, communication seems to be no problem for children. Birgit was able to convey all she wanted during her stay.

After three days she was discharged. The diagnosis was a minor concussion. We were asked to give the child some rest and to come back for a final check-up in four days' time.

Now, when I wanted to pay, I heard that because of the N.H.S. everything was free! All we could do was give a box of chocolates to the nurses who had looked after her. Of course, you as British taxpayers have contributed to this generosity, too. Therefore

	How does the visitor feel about the treatment given to his daughter? Tick the correct answer.	a very unsatisfied ☐
		b only just satisfied ☐
		c satisfied ☐
		d happy ☐
		e very happy ☐

3.1 Make some short notes.
   a cause of Birgit's admission to hospital
   b symptoms
   c diagnosis
   d treatment

3.2 Groupwork

Form groups of three. Imagine your group contains Birgit's mother, who says what happened, the G.P., and Birgit's father, who offers to take Birgit to hospital himself. Can you act the scene? When you have finished, listen to the actual conversation on the tape.

3.3 Make some short notes again.

   a What were Birgit's parents told after the X-rays had been taken?
   b What was Birgit's father's reaction?
   c What was the male nurse worried about?
   d What was his solution to the problem?
   e What did Birgit's father tell him?

3.4 Groupwork

Imagine your group contains the doctor who informs Birgit's parents about the X-rays and what is going to happen, Birgit's father, and the male nurse on night duty. Can you act the two scenes? When you have finished, listen to the actual conversation.

3.5 What do you think the writer was going to say at the end of his letter?
'Therefore …

You may like one of the following suggestions.

'I hope that when you come to visit us, you will have to be taken to hospital, so that we may do something in return for you!'
'… may I kindly offer to pay your N.H.S. contributions for one year?'

What other suggestions do you have, and why?

4 Now listen to these brief comments about the N.H.S. For each one say whether the speaker is favourable or unfavourable to it. Discuss your answers with a partner.

	1	2	3	4	5	6
favourable						
unfavourable						
mixed						

4.1 Now listen again. This time note down the reasons each person gives for his/her opinion. Again discuss your notes with a partner.

5 Now read this newspaper extract and look at the table. Do you still think the N.H.S. is wonderful? Discuss your ideas with a partner.

THE SUNDAY TIMES, 31 AUGUST 1980

How the other half dies

THE Working Group on Inequalities in Health began its work in 1977 with the belief, shared by most of us, that the noble aim of the founders of the National Health Service – to make free health care available to everyone everywhere – had been largely achieved. It did not take the members long to realize that something had gone seriously wrong.

They took statistics at the start of the National Health Service, another set for 1970–72, and the most recent available, and compared them using the system of dividing the population into occupational classes.

They are: Class I: professionals such as doctors, lawyers and accountants. Class II: people like managers, schoolteachers and nurses. Class III: secretaries, shop-assistants, butchers, carpenters. Class IV: agricultural workers, bus-conductors, postmen. Class V: labourers, cleaners, dock workers.

The group was alarmed to find that if you are a labourer, cleaner or a dock worker you are twice as likely to die than a member of the professional classes. You are more likely to have respiratory disease, infectious disease, and trouble with your nervous, circulatory and digestive systems. You are more likely to get cancer and more likely to suffer from mental illness. And – with the exception of mental illness – so is your wife.

Your child is twice as likely to die at birth and during the first month of life, and four times as likely to die in the next 11 months. He is more likely to be ill, especially with respiratory diseases, and far more likely to be injured or killed in an accident, both in and out of the home. He is more likely also to suffer ill health at all stages of his life, especially long term sickness and disability.

And not only did the figures show that there had been no improvement in the situation over the past 33 years, in some aspects the health of the lower social classes had deteriorated.

THE MORTALITY RATES – JOB BY JOB

The tables below show the death rate per 1,000 of men aged 15-64 in different occupations

● HIGH DEATH-RATE		● LOW DEATH-RATE	
Coal miners (underground)	8.22	University teachers	2.87
Shoemakers, and shoe repairers	8.98	Physiotherapists	2.97
Leather products makers	8.95	Paper products makers	3.02
Machine tool operators	9.34	Managers in building and contracting	3.19
Watch repairers	9.46	Local authority senior officers	3.42
Coal miners (above ground)	9.72	Ministers of the Crown, MPs, senior	
Steel erectors, riggers	9.92	government officials	3.71
Fishermen	10.28	Primary and secondary school teachers	3.96
Labourers and unskilled workers, all		Sales managers	4.21
industries	12.47	Architects, town planners	4.43
Policemen	12.70	Civil service executive officers	4.67
Bricklayers' labourers	16.44	Postmen	4.84
Electrical engineers	19.04	Medical practitioners	4.94

8
Self-defence

1 **Test yourself!**

Try the following quiz. It will tell you how violent and aggressive you are.

A You are alone for the night and hear a knock at the door at eleven o'clock. Would you
  a open the door to see who is there?
  b call the police?
  c not make any noise and pretend you're not at home?
  d not open the door, but ask who it is?

B You have just been burgled. Would you
  a think it happens to everybody once in a while and not do anything about it?
  b move to another, safer flat/house?
  c decide to do something to prevent a second burglary?
  d find out who did it, so that you can avenge yourself?

C You come back late at night and find a man standing around near your house. Would you
  a ask him what he's doing there?
  b rush back home and lock yourself in?
  c go to some neighbours instead of going home and ask them to accompany you home?
  d get back home, watch him out of the window, and phone the police if he doesn't go?

D Somebody has broken into your house and you decide to install a new protection system. Would you choose
  a a new set of locks?
  b a watch-dog?
  c a gun?
  d a burglar-alarm?

E Some noisy children are constantly coming into your garden to steal your apples. Would you
  a keep telling them to go away?
  b threaten to tell their parents?
  c put up a wooden fence round your garden?
  d put up an iron fence with spikes to make sure they can't get in?

F Someone suggests to you that you put a booby trap* in your home when you are away. What would your reaction be? Would you
  a agree, put one in, and put up a sign to warn the burglars?
  b agree and put one in?
  c say you'll think about it?
  d reject the suggestion?

G You have lost your wallet and you suspect that somebody who works with you has taken it. Would you
  a think you're not sure and forget about it?
  b steal his wallet the next day, hoping it contains as much money as yours did?
  c decide to ask him to give it back to you?
  d threaten to tell your boss?

H You are walking alone at night and see a man trying to climb over a fence to get into some private property. You know there is a sign somewhere that says: 'Keep off – DANGER'. Would you
  a rush to the man to tell him he may be doing something dangerous?
  b walk on, because it's none of your business?
  c walk on, thinking that if anything happens, the man deserves it?
  d rush to the police so that they can handle the situation quickly?

I Which of these weapons would you prefer to keep at home
  a a loaded gun (thinking you'll never pull the trigger, anyway)?
  b a toy pistol (just to frighten the burglar)?
  c an unloaded gun (just to frighten the burglar)?
  d a loaded gun (thinking you might have to use it to defend yourself)?

* an apparently harmless object that will kill or injure somebody when it is picked up or interfered with.

J   Do you think burglars and thieves
   a   usually get the punishment they deserve when they are caught?
   b   should be kept in prison much longer?
   c   should be kept in prison much longer – then forced to work to pay back what they have stolen?
   d   should be helped rather than put into prison?

K   There have been several burglaries in the neighbourhood. Which of the following solutions would you adopt?

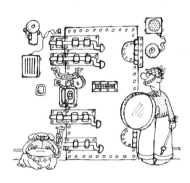

a

b

c

When you have finished, compare your answers with your partner. Then look at the interpretation of your score below.

How to score:

A   a = 1   b = 2   c = 4   d = 3
B   a = 4   b = 3   c = 2   d = 1
C   a = 1   b = 4   c = 3   d = 2
D   a = 4   b = 2   c = 1   d = 3
E   a = 4   b = 3   c = 2   d = 4
F   a = 1   b = 2   c = 3   d = 4
G   a = 4   b = 1   c = 3   d = 2
H   a = 4   b = 2   c = 1   d = 3
I   a = 2   b = 4   c = 3   d = 1
J   a = 4   b = 2   c = 1   d = 3
K   a = 2   b = 3   c = 1

If you get:

under 15   You certainly believe self-defence is necessary. But be careful! This might hide a tendency towards being aggressive yourself.

between 15 and 25   You are firm, determined and ready to stand up for your own rights. You also have a strong sense of the law, but this may sometimes lead you to forget some more humane considerations.

between 25 and 35   You are a very considerate and kind person. Before making any kind of decision, you always think of the consequences it might have for other people. You also tend to be easily frightened.

over 35   You hate violence. You are very frightened generally and tend to avoid facing problems. You should try to acquire a little more self-assurance.

The Ipswich Chronicle, September 14th

SELF-DEFENCE DRAMA

A MAN was seriously injured last night as he was breaking into Mr David Arden's country house in Lowbridge, Suffolk. A booby trap went off just as he was entering the office where the safe and valuables are kept. The burglar, Philip Kingston, was taken to Ipswich Hospital but his life was not in danger.

Mrs Princeton, who lives next door to Templeton House where the drama took place, heard an explosion and screams at 11.30 last night. 'I knew it must have come from Mr Arden's house,' she said. 'He's the only neighbour we have, and although there is a brick wall separating the gardens, the two houses are really very near. I called my husband. He'd heard the screams too, so we decided to phone the police. I was afraid to go and see for myself: the gate is always locked anyway and Mr Arden doesn't much like anybody getting into his garden. He's got spikes all over the wall along the street and there's a sign that says 'danger' . . .'

The police arrived ten minutes later and found that the front gate had been forced open. The house is situated at the bottom of a large garden and when they got in they found Kingston lying near the door that leads from the hall into the study. Apparently a bomb had exploded as he opened the study door, the first room on the right inside the house.

Police stated that Mr Arden's house had already been burgled several times and the booby trap which exploded had probably been put there quite recently to prevent a new attempt. Police are now trying to contact Mr Arden who normally lives in London, and is away on a business trip to the continent.

2.1 A journalist from a local paper in Norwich phoned the police-station in Lowbridge to get some information about what had happened. Unfortunately the line was very bad and he did not get the facts very clearly. Can you list all the mistakes he made in the short article he wrote for his newspaper? Compare your answers with your partner.

DRAMA IN LOWBRIDGE

LATE last night, police in Lowbridge were alerted by a passer-by who heard screams coming from Mr Arden's house. On investigation, they discovered that the house had been broken into, causing a booby trap to go off. The burglar, Philip Kingston, was lying in the study, seriously injured.

Mr Arden, the owner of the house, who was in London, has been arrested on a charge of manslaughter.

Neighbours say it is the first burglary that has taken place in the neighbourhood.

Instead of	It should be
passer-by	*neighbour*

2.2 Can you tell which of the following maps corresponds to the description given in the article? When you have decided, explain why you chose it to your partner.

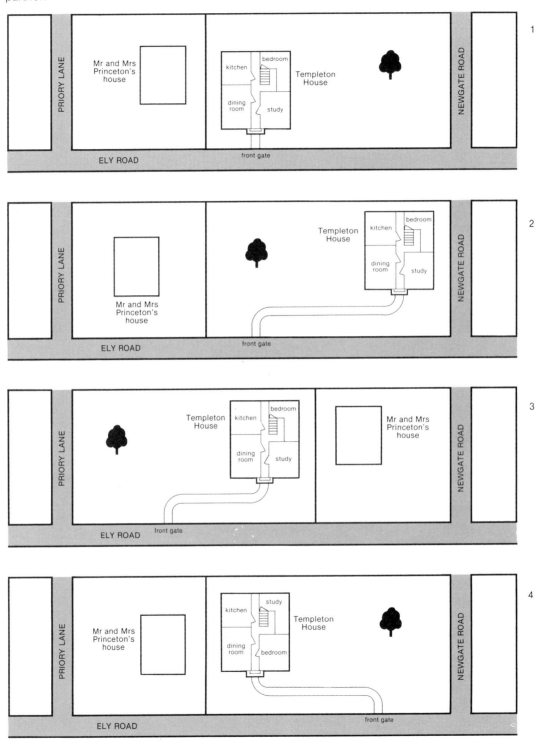

3   Some time after reading the article, you receive a letter saying that you have been chosen as a member of the jury for Mr Arden's trial. He is accused of being responsible for Philip Kingston's injuries. You will be asked to decide whether or not you think Mr Arden is guilty.

On the following pages, you will find a number of texts and documents giving more details about the facts and the personalities of the two men. You will have to decide which ones add to the arguments against them and which ones, on the contrary, tend to lessen their responsibility. After reading and listening to this material, you should be able to make up your mind. When you are reading the next pages, write down your notes and impressions: it will help you to come to a decision more quickly afterwards. Do not make a final decision until you have gone through all the documents.

3.1

```
                    INFORMATION SHEET

    NAME:  ARDEN David George ..............

    BORN IN  Southampton ..........  ON  June 11 1925 ......

    ADDRESS:  41, St Andrew's Walk, Kensington .................

    FAMILY SITUATION:  married — one son, Jonathan ...........

    PROFESSION:  Interior Decorator ....................
```

3.2

```
TEMPLETON HOUSE

Has been in Mr Arden's family for four generations, since
1806. As an interior decorator, Mr Arden has done a lot to
improve the house. It contains valuable antiques and paintings.
Mr Arden has recently acquired some valuable antique china
which he keeps in his house.

The house was broken into in 1977 and several very valuable
paintings were stolen. Mr Arden had new security locks put in,
but just one year later, the same thing happened. This time
some beautiful silver and jewellery were taken away. It was
then that Mr Arden decided to leave the most valuable things
in a safe in his study and to put a booby trap on the door.
```

3.3 Below, you will find a list of events in Mr Kingston's life. How would you tell a friend about his life? (Make sure you use the right tense.)

1939 Nov. 4th, born in New York.
1962 Gets married.
1966 Birth of son, Ben.
1968 Wife starts working in supermarket as an assistant. Still works there.
1970 Birth of daughter, Lesley.
1972 Move to Southend. Takes new job in garage.
1976 Caught stealing from shop.
1977 Steals from department store. One month in jail.
1978 Breaks into shop at night. Arrested with two friends.
1978 Nov. sent to prison.
1979 Feb. let out of prison. No job. Rarely goes to see his wife and children.

3.4 Mr Arden and Mr Kingston were interviewed as they came out of court. Listen to their justifications and fill in a table like the following.

	justifications	the effect of the sign	the future
Mr Kingston			
Mr Arden			

62   *Self-defence*

3.5 Some other examples

In Cordele, Ga. (pop. 12,100) for example, the local prosecutor did not see fit to bring a charge of manslaughter against a store owner who responded to small thefts from his cigarette machine by boobytrapping it after business hours with dynamite, an act that resulted in the death of a teenaged tamperer. But a court awarded civil damages to the boy's mother.

In a 1971 Iowa case, *Katko* vs. *Briney*, the State Supreme Court upheld an award of $30,000 in damages to a man who was injured by a spring-gun when he broke into the upstairs bedroom of an abandoned farmhouse.

In a 1974 case, San Anselmo, Calif., Homeowner Don Luis Ceballos was convicted of assault with a deadly weapon when his spring-gun shot a teenager who tried to steal some musical instruments from his garage.

FATAL MISTAKE

IN MANCHESTER last night, a man seriously injured his 17-year-old son, mistaking him for a burglar. There had been several burglaries in the neighbourhood lately and when Mr Brian Eliot heard a noise, he did not hesitate a second but took his shotgun and went downstairs. When he saw something moving in the living-room, he fired. Mr Eliot's son was rushed to Manchester General Hospital and is said to be in a critical condition.

3.6 Some opinions

Look at the following opinions that appeared in the Ipswich Chronicle. Arrange them in order of approval of Mr Arden's action. Compare your answers with your partner.

approval
↓
disapproval

a

Dear Sir,
I was shocked to read in your paper that some people seem to pity Mr Kingston and blame Mr Arden for the accident. I think every citizen has the right to defend his own property. If criminals choose to damage our homes, why should we feel obliged to find excuses for them? If anything happens to them, they only get what they deserve.
Yours sincerely,
Edna Briars
Debenham

b

Dear Sir,
In an age of aggressiveness, it seems to me extremely dangerous to consider Mr Arden's attitude as normal. I can certainly understand his anger, but violence is surely not the best way of dealing with violence. For where would we stop?
Yours sincerely,
Ann Shepherd
Woodbridge

c

Dear Sir,
I cannot see how Mr Arden can be responsible for the accident that took place in his house. I think that all house owners should be *encouraged* to set booby traps in their houses when they are away. If only we had the courage to follow his example there would certainly be less criminality.
Yours sincerely,
Patrick Rosewood
Colchester

3.7 Now note down the arguments for and against Mr Arden and Mr Kingston on the table your teacher will give you. Work in pairs to decide whether your verdict is guilty or not guilty.

4 Further reading

Read the following article from *Newsweek* and compare it with what happened to Mr Arden and Mr Kingston. You will be given a grid to complete. When you have finished, compare it with a partner.

Burgled French cottage with warning sign; inset: owner Lionel Legras

Burglars and Booby Traps

To catch a thief, don't use a spring-gun

The isolated country cottage in the Aube region of northeastern France was easy pickings for burglars, who regularly made off with furniture, children's toys, sheets and kitchenware. After a dozen such thefts, owner Lionel Legras, 50, operator of a local garage, fastened some shotgun cartridges to the inside of a transistor radio and locked it in a cupboard; he wired it to a timer that would detonate the shells 90 seconds after the radio was moved or switched on. Outside, he posted a warning: ENTRY PROHIBITED, DANGER. EXPLOSIVE DEVICES.

One evening in 1976, woodcutters René Vermeulen, 31, and André Rousseau, 30, climbed over the fence outside Legras' cottage, forced open a door and broke into the cupboard. Vermeulen turned the radio on, and the cartridges exploded. He was thrown to the floor, his chest ripped open and his right hand blown away; Rousseau, partially blinded, went for help. Vermeulen died; Rousseau, one eye permanently damaged, was charged with attempted burglary.

Rousseau then took a step that raised the case from a local incident to a French *cause célèbre*: he filed suit against Legras, seeking $22,000 in damages. Even more galling, as many Frenchmen saw it, he nearly got his way. After a month-long dual trial, a court let Burglar Rousseau off with a two-month suspended sentence. As for owner Legras, however, while no damages were assessed against him, he was declared guilty of using excessive force to defend his home. His sentence: eight months, suspended.

9

Plan your new town

1 The following pages describe a problem which you will have to solve. It is about town-planning. In order to find a solution, you will have several things to do:

a Understand the present situation in the town and the problem.
b Discuss what should be done.
c Note other people's opinions.

To do this, you will:

- read some letters to the editor of a newspaper
- listen to some suggestions on the tape
- read a newspaper article relating to the problem

When you have gone through this, you will be able to consider the advantages and disadvantages of the various possibilities and make a decision.

The problem

The small community in which you live (near the intersection of the Oxford–Northampton road and of the main London–Birmingham road) used to be a district of the neighbouring town of Glasford. But recently it has become independent. It is now called Fulston. The voters of Fulston have elected their councillors and you are one of them. You have one transitional year during which you can still use the services and facilities (the schools, hospitals, and so on) of Glasford. You will then become independent and gradually move into your own public buildings. It is now urgent to start building some of them. As the amount of money you have is limited, you must decide what your priorities are. In fact, your main problem is to decide what land you should buy to build on. Once you have bought the land, you will be able to borrow the money necessary for building on it.

Your town has been granted a total of £400,000 to buy land, so you will have to decide:

What land to buy with the money you have

Only a few plots of land are for sale. They are the blank plots on the map (page 66). You may decide to buy only some of them if you wish. Some areas, as you will see, are cheaper than others. But it is not always a good policy to buy cheaper land if it brings problems later on.

What to build where

Following the map is a list of all the suggestions so far. (For the sake of convenience, the plots for sale on the map have been divided into squares which are all of the same size.)

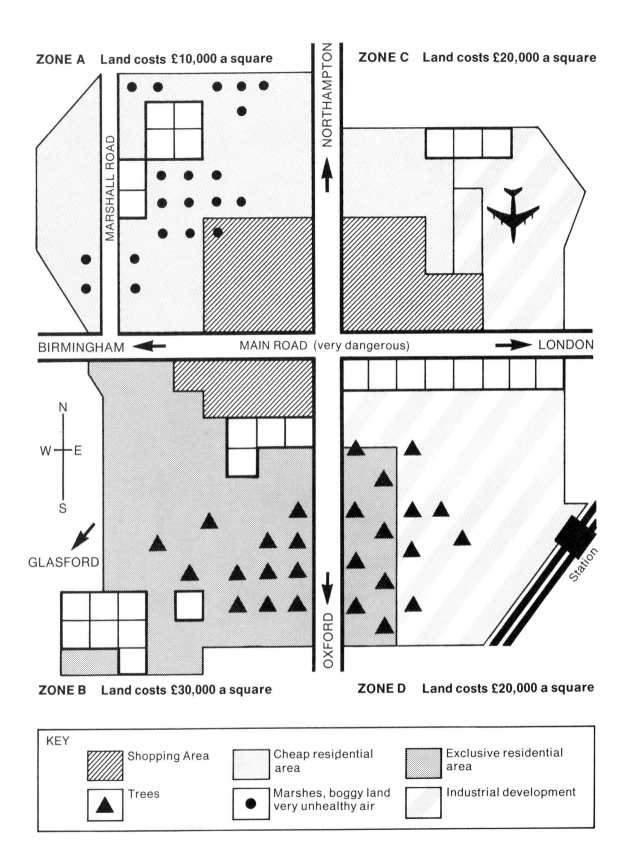

ZONE A Land costs £10,000 a square

ZONE C Land costs £20,000 a square

NORTHAMPTON

MARSHALL ROAD

BIRMINGHAM ← MAIN ROAD (very dangerous) → LONDON

N
W ─┼─ E
S

GLASFORD

ZONE B Land costs £30,000 a square

OXFORD

Station

ZONE D Land costs £20,000 a square

KEY

Shopping Area

Trees

Cheap residential area

Marshes, boggy land very unhealthy air

Exclusive residential area

Industrial development

buildings	area necessary*
Secondary School	6 squares
Home for Old People	1 square
Kindergarten	1 square
Sports Centre	4 squares
Town Hall	4 squares
Primary School	2 squares
Hospital	6 squares
Arts and Cultural Centre	2 squares
Council Houses	4 squares or more

* It is impossible to change these conditions as you can only work with one firm of architects and they already have some plans.

2 Your opinion

2.1 Do you wish to add anything to the above list of suggestions? If you do, how many squares do you think it would require?

2.2 List all the suggestions in order of priority.

2.3 In the list below, you will find expressions which you can use to talk about some of the buildings or amenities. Match the buildings with these expressions, using the following structures:

Ideally, a school should be in a safe area.
Ideally, a .... needs to have ....
Ideally, a .... should be ....

- *quiet*
- *next to ...*
- *not far from ...*
- *in a safe area easily accessible*
- *clean atmosphere*
- *right in the centre of the town*
- *in a residential district*

Can you add to the list of expressions?

2.4 Now look at the map and consider each of the areas in each zone in terms of:

- size
- shape
- situation
- zone
- price   etc.

You will find that most of them have advantages and disadvantages. Try to explain this to your partner using the following expressions:

A good thing is that ...	*but ...*
One of the advantages ...	*On the other hand, ...*
What's good about ...	*Unfortunately, ...*
What I like about ...	*Yet, ...*
It's perfect as far as ... is concerned	*But ... don't forget ...*
Another advantage ...	*Another disadvantage ...*

2.5 Now with your partner compare some of the areas. Use some of these adjectives/prepositions.

cheap	small	dangerous
expensive	exclusive	healthy
big	noisy	unhealthy
far from ...	near ...	

For example: *It's near to the shops ...*
It costs twice as much as ...
It looks more/less dangerous than ...

3 Public opinion

3.1

THE FULSTON NEWS

Letters

Dear Sir,
I would like to draw your attention to the condition of old people in our town. Many of them live in miserable conditions, not only because their homes are not very cheerful, but mainly because no one cares about them. Anything could happen to them at any time. The recent case of Mrs Levinson, who would have died after a fall if a neighbour hadn't happened to visit her, is a sad example of the way we neglect the older generation in our community. It is high time we did something. We should have a home offering rooms, treatment, and various activities. There isn't even one in Glasford! I hope we will fill this need in Fulston and have a community we can be proud of.
Yours sincerely,
P Barns,
Fulston.

Dear Sir,
We have just moved to Fulston after living for ten years in the north of England. Although we like this community very much, we are really disappointed at the lack of sports facilities around here. My husband, who plays football and was a member of our local team, has had to stop playing, and there isn't even a sports centre where he can practise athletics! I suggest that we build sports facilities in Fulston, including, of course, a swimming-pool. As well as answering a basic human need, these might keep the youth of Fulston off the streets, and I am sure many of your readers will agree with me.
Yours sincerely,
Mrs A James,
Fulston.

Dear Sir,
I am a mother of four children aged 5 to 14 and I think it's a real shame the school system is so poor. We live in the north of Fulston, near Marshall Road and my daughter, who is 14, has to travel three-quarters of an hour every day to go to Glasford Comprehensive School. What do you think you are doing to our children? It's all right for those families who live to the south; their children only have one bus to take. But why is it that we, in the poorer districts always have to put up with all the problems? Why not build the new school in the vacant area near Marshall Road? The area may not be ideal, but *we* live there all day long, we have no choice. So why couldn't some other children spend a few hours here every day?
Yours sincerely,
Joan Bratford,
6, Long Road,
Fulston.

Read the above letters carefully and make a list of the words and phrases expressing complaint, or making suggestions. Which possible buildings do these letters refer to? How could they influence your decision? Write down your remarks in the table your teacher will give you .

3.2 Before making your choice, you received this letter. Unfortunately, some drops of water ran onto it as it was raining hard, and you can't read it. You feel it might be important and ask your secretary to phone Mrs Chambers. Listen to what she says and complete the letter according to the information she gives.

Mrs A. Chambers
The Fulston Parents' Association
11 Finchley Road, Fulston
Tel: Fulston 9034

Dear Sir,
After the last meeting of ⬛⬛⬛ation which was held last Tuesday in ⬛⬛⬛ we wish to express ⬛⬛⬛ that Fulston's new secondary school might ⬛⬛⬛ London to Birmingham road. We know that ⬛⬛⬛ has been decided yet, but we are aware that a piece of ⬛⬛⬛ is for there. ⬛⬛⬛ we feel the urg⬛⬛⬛ drawing your attention to the ⬛⬛⬛ this area would ⬛⬛⬛ for our future school.
1) It is ⬛⬛⬛ from the main residential ⬛⬛⬛ in Fulston and would therefore imply a long ⬛⬛⬛ for most of our children.
2) The ⬛⬛⬛ (mainly in ⬛⬛⬛) is certainly not suitable for a school.
3) The main ⬛⬛⬛ against such a project is the ⬛⬛⬛ to the main London to Birmingham road. During the ⬛⬛⬛ months, one child was killed on this road, and three injured. What would this number be if the children had to walk along this road every day to go to school?
We are confident that you will take these points into consideration and thank you in anticipation.

Yours sincerely,
A. Chambers

3.3   Many people in Fulston were asked what they considered most important for
       their new town. Listen to what three of them said and complete the grid your
       teacher will give you.

3.4   Read the following article and, discuss with your partner how it relates to the
       problem of what to build (and where) in Fulston.

A MENACE TO PUBLIC HEALTH?

MR & MRS DOUGLAS, of 23 Pemberley Road, Fulston, were taken to Glasford hospital last night after contracting a lung infection. This is the sixth similar case in Fulston since last July and doctors think the disease might be related to the atmospheric pollution in the north-western part of the town where all six people came from. Most of the district east of Marshall Road is built on low-lying land and there is frequent mist and smog in this part of the town. Doctors have warned of the danger which living in such an area could represent, especially for young children and old people. They have alerted the authorities and an enquiry has been requested.

4.1   You now have the information you need to make your choice. Consider each of
       the projects you want to build and discuss its advantages and disadvantages,
       using the following structure:

       If the school is built ..., it will be perfect for ... but it will cost ... .
       If we spend ... on ..., nothing will be left for ... .
       If we don't build a ..., parents/people ... will ... .

4.2   You can now note down all the information in the grid you were given earlier.

Your final choice

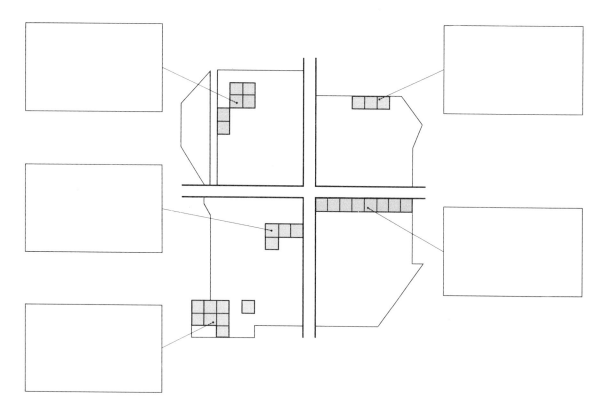

5.1 If your project has been accepted, it probably works quite well. But, imagine that one of your friend's projects was chosen instead. You do not agree with it, and know it will lead to problems. Write a typical letter of complaint to your friend.

5.2 You have thought about a plan for Fulston. Think about the town you live in. Has it got similar problems? Can you think of a new public building that should be built somewhere? Or can you find examples of bad town-planning?

10
The outsiders

1 Not everyone in Great Britain is as happy about the National Health Service as the foreign visitor in Unit 7. Listen to part of a conversation between a journalist and some tramps in Dr Aylin's waiting room. How many people can you hear? (You will read more about Dr Aylin and his patients afterwards.)

Listen again to parts of the conversation and answer the following questions.

1.1 Try to say whether the following statements are true or false.
The first patient:

	true	false
a People saw them when they were ill, but did not help them.	☐	☐
b People heard about them only when they died in hospital.	☐	☐
c People heard about them when it was too late to do anything for them.	☐	☐

1.2 Tick the best answer.
The second patient said:

a People think 'the only good tramp is a dead tramp'. ☐
b People are just not interested in us. ☐
c People are not interested and do not want to hear about us either! ☐

1.3 What does the first patient tell us about the attitude of the hospital staff?
They .... because ....

1.4 The third patient (Brian):
What happened to him and what part did Dr Aylin play in it?
Tick the correct answer(s):

a Brian was taken back home by Dr Aylin. ☐
b Brian was admitted to hospital. ☐
c Brian stayed in hospital for more than a week. ☐
d Dr Aylin remained very calm. ☐
e Dr Aylin got very angry. ☐
f Dr Aylin told the hospital staff they had to admit Brian. ☐

1.5 The second patient:
What information does he give about the doctor and the tramp at the end of the interview? (Do not listen only to what is actually said, but also to what is suggested.)

Tick off the correct answer(s):

Dr Aylin:		Tramps:	
a is honest.	☐	a know they are 'different'.	☐
b is strict.	☐	b don't mind when the doctor's drunk.	☐
c is marvellous.	☐	c sometimes have a few drinks.	☐
d likes a few drinks himself.	☐	d only drink when it's cold.	☐

1.6 Can you now summarize the information you have on the situation in Dr Aylin's waiting room? (Who? Where? When? Why? How?)

1.7 Write down some questions about things you still have no information on but which you would like to know about.

2 Read the following newspaper article in an English newspaper. Does it answer any of the questions you asked?

DR DAVID AYLIN, 36, dressed in a suit, moves into his waiting-room. It's a bare room decorated with a few Jesus posters. Sitting in rows on battered chairs are Dr Aylin's 'patients'.

They are about 50 in number, hardly speak to each other, and scarcely look up. The only thing they have in common is suspicion of everyone else and a 'uniform' – clothes unwashed and grey with use. They are the hidden victims of inner-city change. Twenty years ago a Birmingham man with a few pennies in his hand could find a lodging-house, hostel, or cheap hotel. Then came development. The city got a new concrete-and-glass heart and it was hoped the tramps would disappear. But they didn't.

They have stayed although they have no shelter. They come to Dr Aylin's waiting-room, where for the price of a prayer the men receive soup, bread and tea, plus in the last eighteen months the care of a family doctor.

Dr Aylin comes into the waiting-room and gets straight down to business. If anyone wants to see him, he says, they can make their way down to the surgery at the end of the alley. As the rest eat, three of them come. John, a youth still, but who looks like a middle-aged man, has a poisoned finger. Bill, living rough, is having trouble sleeping. A third young man is crippled by sciatica.

Down-and-outs, as all these men are, often suffer from T.B., foot and chest infections and the side-effects of alcoholism. But when their only address is an empty house or alley, complications build up fast.

'I don't treat people here as special cases', Dr Aylin explains. 'They are just patients who have certain rights and need some respect and who should receive the same benefit from the National Health Service as anybody else.'

In 18 months Dr Aylin has seen 92 men and 3 women and given 180 consultations. He wants to extend the service. He would like to be open seven nights a week and provide nurses, consultants, and more doctors too. But the local authorities have turned down his request for money. Birmingham like every city in the country sees little need to do something for these grey shadows, who officially, do not seem to exist.

3 Do the following work in your groups. You can look at the text of the article on page 73 as often as you need.

3.1 These nameless people are referred to in various ways for these different reasons:

a They do not seem to exist.
b They walk long distances and have no home.
c They are at the bottom of the social scale.
d Dr Aylin does not treat them as special cases.
e Few people know how the changes of the inner-city affected them.

Can you say what they are called, and in each case give one of the reasons?

	name	reason
1	*grey shadows*	*a*
2		
3		
4		
5		

3.2 Work in your groups, and make brief notes on one or more of the following elements in this story.

information given	Dr Aylin personal data clothes movements whom does he meet what does he say plans for future	The waiting-room	Patients personal data housing clothes	Birmingham situation 20 years ago changes effect of changes on tramps
brief notes				

3.3 Imagine you are a reporter in a television documentary programme on 'Dr Aylin and his Birmingham tramps'.

a First tell the audience something about:
  • Dr Aylin himself
  • his waiting-room
  • his patients
  • the changes in Birmingham

b Then have a short interview with him.

c Finally add your personal comment on how you feel about all this and what ought to be done. The following language might be useful:

We feel …	ought to …
We think …	should …
It seems to us …	are obliged …
We believe …	must …

Use the following script of the documentary:

A.T.V. Studios

Script:
Dr AYLIN AND HIS BIRMINGHAM TRAMPS

SCENE 1 Shot of new centre in
Birmingham.
Camera zooms in on old
building:
Dr Aylin's Clinic.

SCENE 2 Dr Aylin approaches
his new clinic.

SCENE 3 Shot of waiting-room.
Camera zooms in on
Jesus Poster, then on
battered chair...

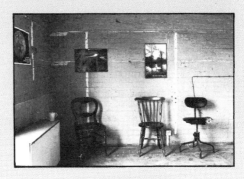

SCENE 4 Patients are shown in
their "uniforms"
eating soup.

SCENE 5   Dr Aylin enters room,
          – speaks to patients
          – walks on to surgery

SCENE 6   Reporter interviews
          Dr Aylin in his
          surgery.

SCENE 7   Reporter in studio.

Now check your work by listening to the documentary on the tape.

4 Caravans next-door

In most countries we find minority-groups that do not fit easily into the pattern of society. One example is the group of tinkers, people that travel from place to place and repair kettles, pans, and so on; another the Gypsies, originally Asiatic people, who move about in caravans and live by collecting scrap-material, horse-dealing, fortune-telling and basket-making. And there are other people, who for one reason or another do not want to dwell in houses, but prefer caravans.

In some countries people have realized they should do something for these people, who feel isolated and discriminated against in their camps, often on the outskirts of towns and villages near the rubbish-dumps. They think a number of large centres with special schools and health centres of their own would be the best solution.

Others think that every town or village should construct a smaller site not far away from its centre, so that the caravan dwellers can take part in the community's life.

4.1 Can you list a number of ideas people in your area have about caravans in general? Can you also give a few reasons why they think so?

4.2 Imagine your municipality has agreed to build a site for fifteen caravans in a park near the centre.

a Can you list a number of disadvantages for the community and for the caravan dwellers themselves?
b Can you list a number of advantages for the community and for the caravan dwellers?

	caravan dwellers	community
disadvantages		
advantages		

4.3 Imagine you are one of these caravan dwellers and you read the following letter in the local paper:

> Sir,
>
> Now that the municipality has decided to construct a site for fifteen caravans in Hatley Park, I would like to make the following suggestions:
>
> 1 Police patrols in the area should be increased.
>
> 2 The building of a small separate school seems inevitable if we do not wish to have our children mix with dirty and unruly gypsy children.
>
> 3 The local health authorities should carry out regular checks on the hygiene on the site.
>
> 4 There should be a strict control on the number of people allowed to live together in one caravan.
>
> 5 House owners in the area should be compensated for the fall in value of their property.
>
> 6 In a year's time there should be a local referendum to decide whether the site should continue or not.
>
> Why should it always be the decent, law-abiding citizens who have to suffer?
>
> Yours faithfully,
> **Norman A Hogg**

Choose one of the following assignments:

a Write a letter to Mr Hogg in which you explain politely how sad you feel about his letter. Tell him you want to belong to a community. Apologize for not being able to write English as well as he does, because you did not go to a good school. Explain that everyone needs a place to live in.

b With the members of your group make an information leaflet which is going to be distributed among the people of this town. Explain why caravan dwellers are different, but not second-rate citizens. Tell them you understand people who write letters like the one by Mr Hogg, but they are the result of prejudice. In fact caravan dwellers are usually very honest people, who respect the law and try to make a living by working. It is simply that people are intolerant and afraid of people who are 'different'. Indicate also what sort of photographs you would like to have in the leaflet.

c Draw or paint a poster or make a collage which expresses these same feelings.

d Read the following poem by an African writer and with your group compose a similar poem about being an outsider of a different kind.

Telephone Conversation

The price seemed reasonable, location
Indifferent. The landlady swore she lived
Off premises. Nothing remained
But self-confession. 'Madam', I warned,
'I hate a wasted journey – I am African.'
Silence. Silenced transmission of
Pressurized good breeding. Voice, when it came,
Lipstick coated, long gold-rolled
Cigarette-holder pipped. Caught I was, foully.
'HOW DARK?' ... I had not misheard ... 'ARE YOU LIGHT
OR VERY DARK?' Button B. Button A. Stench
Of rancid breath of public hide-and-speak.
Red booth. Red pillar-box. Red double-tiered
Omnibus squelching tar. It was real! Shamed
By ill-mannered silence, surrender
Pushed dumbfounded to beg simplification.
Considerate she was, varying the emphasis –
'ARE YOU DARK? OR VERY LIGHT?' Revelation came.
'You mean – like plain or milk chocolate?'
Her assent was clinical, crushing in its light
Impersonality. Rapidly, wave-length adjusted,
I chose. 'West African sepia' – and as afterthought,
'Down in my passport.' Silence for spectroscopic
Flight of fancy, till truthfulness clanged her accent
Hard on the mouthpiece. 'WHAT'S THAT?' conceding
'DON'T KNOW WHAT THAT IS.' 'Like brunette.'
'THAT'S DARK, ISN'T IT?' 'Not altogether.
Facially, I am brunette, but madam, you should see
The rest of me. Palm of my hand, soles of my feet
Are a peroxide blonde. Friction, caused –
Foolishly madam – by sitting down, has turned
My bottom raven black – One moment madam!' – sensing
Her receiver rearing on the thunderclap
About my ears – 'Madam,' I pleaded, 'wouldn't you rather
See for yourself?'

Wole Soyinka ©

11
An inside job

1 Four people have decided to break into a bank and steal the money kept in the safe. All four live in Canterbury or nearby, and they have chosen one of the branches of the Kentish Bank, in Dover Street, partly because Joe Rivers has been working there as a clerk for the past four years.

Joe Rivers 34. Works in the Kentish Bank as a clerk.

Brenda Tillotson 26. Joe's girlfriend. A trainee teacher.

Bert Westing 38. A mechanic for the Ford dealer, in Canterbury. Married, two children. He once had a job as a welder in a factory.

Dennis Wright 56. Owns a small garage in Ashford. Divorced.

1.1 After listening to and reading this conversation, find out:

a The working hours for staff in the bank.
b The time they decide to break in.
c The date they decide to break in.

First discussion about the robbery

Bert So, I think … I think we're all agreed that it's going to be a quiet job. All right? So that above all …

Brenda Yes, and I think that means at night. Yes?

Dennis No, no, you mean no violence, don't you? Is that what you meant?

Bert I meant no violence. All right, Joe? There's going to be no weapons in this.

Joe Absolutely not. I mean … I …

Bert No stick-ups. Nothing like that.

Dennis Well, we're all agreed on that, I think. Don't you?

Joe Right. Absolutely.

Bert So … umm … I think … umm … we should get in there during the day, quite frankly. I think we should get in there, hang about, see if we can get in the back, in the offices, up a back stair-case or something, hide in there, and get the stuff out during the lunch-break, when there's a lot of people rushing around.

Dennis Yeah, but if there's a lot of people rushing around there's going to be violence, isn't there? I mean, how are we going to …

Bert I'd have thought we'd mingle with the crowd myself, personally.

Joe We can't just walk into a bank. Why not do it at night, when it's all nice and quiet? You've got plenty of time, you've got from five o'clock at night when the bank closes, till nine-thirty in the morning when we all come into work again.

Dennis I agree with Joe, Bert. He's got the right idea.

Bert Night-time?

Dennis Yeah.

Bert Brenda, what do you think?

Brenda Well, I think … umm … if it was possible to do it when the bank was full, you could slip away much easier.

Bert Well, I don't. Well, look, Joe, give us a lay-out of the bank, come on, and then we can work the rest out later.

Joe Right, well … er … now, look, this is to go no further, absolutely not. I'm not really supposed to have this, all right? OK, so we'll take one look at it and then we'll destroy it.

Bert Right.

Joe Now, you come in through the front entrance here. You're faced with a hall where most of the customers … get no further than that. You've got the counters on the right, where people go to deposit their money and so on. Behind the counters there's a safe.

Dennis What's in there, then?

Joe Well, very little. Very little. Er … also facing the front entrance … umm … up beside the counters, there's a long, long corridor.

Bert I see.

Joe On the right-hand side there's three offices …

Bert Yes, slow … slow down, Joe, 'cos I think it's very important. Just take us back. So you come in the door. What do you see when you come in the door of the bank? What's …

Joe Counters on the right, and …

Bert Counters on the right …

Joe … and the corridor facing you …

Bert … and the corr- … and what's on the left?

Joe Er … well, it's just where people go and, you know …

Bert I see, it's a sort of table and chairs and things, is it?

Joe Right … and write their cheques and that. Yeah.

Bert And straight in front's the doorway to the back offices.

Joe Yeah.

Bert Right, got you.

Joe Right … corridor all the way up. Three offices on the right of the corridor … er … the end office has Mr Martin, the Manager, in it. Right?

Bert That's the third one?

Joe That's the third one along on the right.

Bert Yeah.

Joe On the left-hand side there's an office, then the strong-room, and then two more offices.

Bert Office, strong-room, two offices …

Joe But you can only get into the strong-room through the first office. There's no other way in.

Brenda Now that's going up from the hall, is it?

Joe That's from the hall, on the left-hand side.

Bert You all right on that, Dennis?

Dennis Yeah … yeah … I think so. Yeah.

Joe End of that corridor there's the toilets, and then stairs up to the first floor, where my office is.

Brenda Are the offices full all day, all of the offices?

Joe Well, people in and out all the time. I mean …

Brenda So there's no one that's ever empty all day?

Joe No … no.

Bert So this one next to the strong-room, how many's that got in it?

Joe Well, two or … you know, people are passing in and out, putting money in and taking money out, you know.

Dennis Well, you just talked about the toilets. Is it not possible for one of us to go in there … like … and … hide early on … like … in the toilet?

Joe You could do, but you've got a long way to get up that corridor and you've got a long way to get back to the strong-room.

Bert There's no back way into there at all?

Joe No, no. Stairs go straight up to the first floor where I work.

Brenda No windows?

Joe No.

Brenda So that looks like it really has to be a night job, between … umm … somewhere between five p.m. and before nine a.m.

Joe That's right. That's right.

Dennis So really, a weekend … would be … like … most suitable, wouldn't it? Well, there's a long weekend coming up in a month, isn't there? The Easter weekend. So that, if we was to go in on Friday night, we'd have till …

Joe Good Friday!

Dennis Good Friday night. Then we'd … oh, of course, Good Friday, there's no bank on Good Friday, is there? We'd have from Friday … Saturday, Sunday, Monday …

Bert I think Dennis has got a very good point here. I think, really, you know, we've done … said all we can at this stage. I think we should … you know … go away, chew this over, meet again to get into the details of this and …

Joe Let's not hang about. Let's all go …

Bert … same time, same place, then.

Dennis All right.

Bert Righto then. OK.

1.2 Draw a plan of the ground floor of the Kentish Bank. Here is an outline to help you. Your plan should be as detailed as possible.

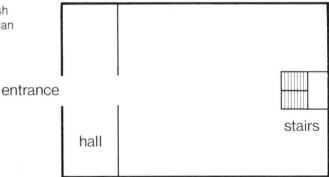

1.3 Read the conversation again and make a list of all the expressions used to make suggestions.

1.4 Look at the plan you have drawn. Can you think of any possibilities you might suggest to Bert, Dennis, Brenda and Joe? Use the expressions you have noted in 1.3 to make these suggestions to your partner.

2 Getting in

Three days later, the four friends met again to discuss how they would actually get into the bank.

2.1 Listen to the recording and look at the diagram on the next page. Mark on the copy you will be given the three routes proposed by Joe, Bert, and Dennis. Use three different colours.

2.2 Indicate with A where the alarm-systems are located. Indicate with B which windows have bars.

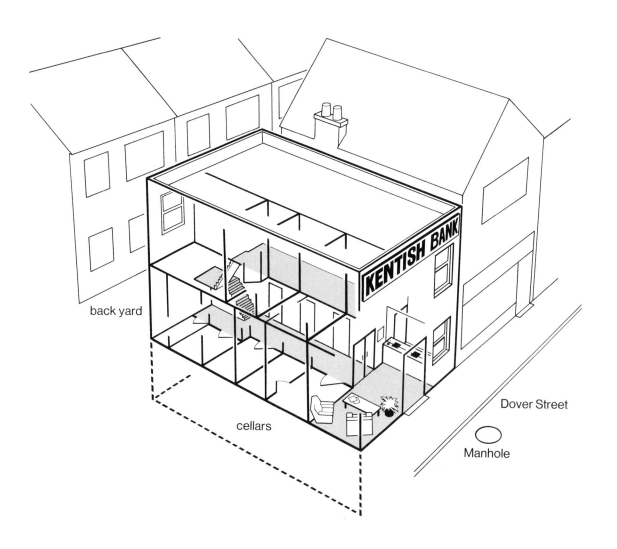

back yard

cellars

KENTISH BANK

Dover Street

Manhole

SECURITY REGULATIONS   The Kentish Bank,
                                        9 Dover Street,
                                        Canterbury.

Each employee will lock the door(s) of his office when
leaving. Those are the only keys he will keep. No one
except the manager and his assistant will have the keys of
the front door. Only the manager will have the keys of the
strong room. He will bring them in every morning. Under no
circumstances are they permitted to be left on the premises.

2.3   Fill in a grid like this.

	drawbacks	advantages
solution proposed by Joe		
solution proposed by Bert		
solution proposed by Dennis		

2.4   Before they separate, Bert, Joe, Brenda, and Dennis again discuss their plans for the night of the robbery. Work in groups of four.

Two of you will list the different steps. For example:
First, we'll get into the back yard and put the ladder against the wall … .
Then … .

The other two will try to think of as many objections as they can. For example:
What if there's somebody in the Temple Street house?
And if …?
But we could … .
Don't you think we'd better …?
Won't it be dangerous to …?

The first two will then try to answer the questions and find ways of solving these problems.

3   **The tools**

The four friends had read this article and decided they would make sure this would not happen to them!

The Daily Gazette, March 20

FORGETFUL THIEVES

Bern, from our correspondent

TWO PEOPLE were caught last night as they were trying to rob a jewellery shop in Alpenstrasse in Bern. They had planned everything carefully but realized when they got into the shop that they had forgotten their bag of tools and master-keys to open the safe where most of the jewels were kept. Both of them are now in the Bern federal prison.

3.1   Here are all the tools they have for the robbery:

a a ladder
b a bunch of master-keys
c a saw
d a pick-axe
e a long rope

f electric wire
g a drill
h a hammer
i gloves
j masks

k dynamite
l torches
m suitcases
n a toy (or unloaded) gun
o a whistle

p shovels
q map of the district
r false papers
s gelignite

Look at the picture below.

a Match the names of the tools and the objects shown in the picture.
b Decide which of these objects they will need and which will not be needed.

tools	picture	needed	not needed
a			
b			
c			
d			
e			
f			
g			
h			
i			
j			
k			
l			
m			
n			
o			
p			
q			
r			
s			

3.2   Look at the objects you have put in the 'needed' column. Explain why they will be needed and how they will be used. Can you think of any more tools they might need? What for?

4   Who does what?

Brenda, Joe, Bert, and Dennis will all have plenty to do on the night of the robbery. But they will have to share out the work.

The driver   This person will have to steal a car just before the robbery, and take it to the bank. After the robbery, he/she will drive the others back to their own car which they will use – if they haven't been followed – to go back to Dennis's flat.

Qualities required: good and fast driving, good knowledge of cars (to choose and deal with the stolen car).

Two men inside They will get into the bank to take the money from the safe.

Qualities required: self-control (they must not panic and react violently if anything goes wrong) and quick reactions. Good physical condition, (it might be necessary to jump, or climb up a rope when leaving the strong-room). One or both must be trained in using the heavy and dangerous equipment necessary to open a safe.

The head This person will act as co-ordinator during the robbery: waiting in the street and warning the others in case of danger, checking the time, making sure they are not followed, and so on. He/she will also decide on any necessary last-minute changes.

Qualities required: a cool head, good eye-sight, ability to take decisions quickly.

Consider the descriptions of the four people given above and the way they reacted during their conversation. Who do you think should do each job? (Do not forget that Joe Rivers is most likely to be suspected since he works in the bank. They should make sure he cannot be suspected.)

5 On the Tuesday that followed the Easter weekend, this article appeared in the Canterbury Evening News:

£30,000 ROBBERY

AT 8.30 this morning, Mr Peter King, a clerk in the Kentish Bank, Dover Street, Canterbury, discovered that the bank had been robbed during the weekend. 'All the money in the safe – £30,000 – has been stolen,' the manager said.

For the past eight years, Mr Peter King has been the first to open the door of the Kentish Bank. His job is to make sure everything is in place by the time everyone arrives, around 8.45 a.m. But when he got there this morning, Mr King had the feeling 'something was wrong'. As he explained later, 'some of the doors which have to be kept shut were open, and one of the first floor windows was open with broken glass all over the floor. I thought of the wind at first, but soon realized it was something far more serious.'

According to the police, the robbers went in through one of the first floor windows and managed to get into the office, which is just above the strong-room. They cut a hole through the floor and using a ladder, reached the strong-room. 'It was an easy way to get in,' the police said. 'But we do have a few clues – some fingerprints, and the ladder, which is of an unusual type and which they must have left behind in their hurry.' The police also think it could have been an inside job.

Police are wondering why the first floor windows in the back had no bars like all the other windows. It seems incredible that such an obvious means of access could have been overlooked. The manager, Mr David Martin, stated that the bank had been about to check the security system.

5.1 Read the article carefully and find out how the actual robbery differed from what had been planned. Use a grid like this.

similarities	differences	
	what had been planned	what happened

5.2 Can you imagine what went wrong and why the four people changed their plans? Consider each of the changes in turn. The following expressions will be useful:

I suppose they …
Something/someone might/could have …
Perhaps …
They may have …

5.3 How do you think the bank manager would complete the following police form?

```
ROBBERY DESCRIPTION SHEET

Names of persons injured or killed: ...........................

Time of robbery: ...........................................

Name of first person on scene: ..............................

Time of discovery: ..........................................

Items stolen: ...............................................

If money, how much: ............   Where from: ..............

Approach used: ..............................................

Escape car seen: ............................................

Description: ................................................

Any suspicious person reported: .............................

Description: ................................................

Inside job: .................................................

Why: ........................................................

Name: .......................................................

Date: .......................................................

Signature: ..................................................

Additional comments: ........................................
```

6 The following article appeared in the Canterbury Evening News, six years later. Does crime ever pay?

Education committee elected

THE YEARLY election of the local education committee took place yesterday. Among the new members are: Mr Joseph Rivers, Manager of the Kentish Bank Dover Street branch; Mrs Brenda Jones, a teacher at St Clare's Comprehensive School; Mr George Callender, engineer; Mr Robert Wasting, a personnel manager; and Mr Dennis Wright, chief of security at Canterbury airport.

The Great Train Robbery

The following article is taken from Newsweek. You should not try to understand every word; the exercise afterwards requires you to follow only the general sense of the text.

The Great Train Robbery

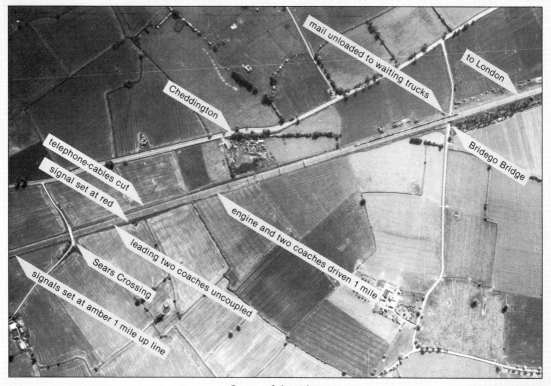

mail unloaded to waiting trucks

to London

Cheddington

Bridego Bridge

telephone-cables cut

signal set at red

engine and two coaches driven 1 mile

leading two coaches uncoupled

Sears Crossing

signals set at amber 1 mile up line

Scene of the crime

Normally Tom Miller wouldn't have bothered. But it was one of those strange English summer nights when a fitful moon lit up the green fields along the railway track and induced a feeling of apprehension. Miller decided to see what was holding up the Royal Mail, the 'Ghost Train' as they call it, that makes the nightly run from Glasgow to London. It had been stopped twenty minutes, longer than any normal signal halt. So the railwayman clambered down from his guards-van at the rear of the train, put lanterns on the track to warn approaching trains, then walked forward. 'Well, you can imagine my surprise when I saw the two coaches and the engine gone,' said Miller, later. Gone, too, was $7 million in cash and diamonds. It was the biggest railroad robbery in history.

It had also been planned with the stopwatch precision of a wartime commando raid. The Royal Mail left Glasgow at 6.50 in the evening. It was not listed in any timetable. As it sped south through the night, 75 skilled General Post Office workers quietly sorted ten coachloads of mail. In coach No. M 30204 M, behind the engine, four unarmed GPO men guarded a packet of diamonds, bundles of registered mail, and two padlocked green cupboards chock-full of worn banknotes destined for destruction by the Bank of England.

At 3.15 a.m. engineer Jack Mills, 58, and his mate, 26-year-old David Whitby, neared the lonely Buckinghamshire hamlet of Cheddington, 40 miles northwest of London. Alongside the signal box at Sears Crossing, where a dirt road crosses the track, fifteen men flattened themselves against the grass and daisies of the railway embankment. They wore blue coveralls. Stockings were pulled over their faces as masks. They carried crowbars, pickaxes, and guns. They had cut every telephone wire in the district and they had rigged a series of signals, covering a green 'go' light with an old glove, setting another at a warning amber, and flashing the red 'stop' sign with flashlight batteries.

Up front on the Royal Mail, engineers Mills and Whitby saw the red signal and brought their 2,000-horsepower diesel to a screeching halt. Whitby recalled later: 'I climbed down and I walked over to the signal box. I found the wires cut, so I went back to tell Jack, and I saw this chap looking at me between the coaches. So I walked over to him and I said, 'What's up, mate?' And he pushed me right down the bank and another bloke grabbed me and put his hand over my mouth. 'If you shout, I'll kill you,' he said. 'I won't shout,' I said. So they took me back and I found they'd coshed my mate, Jack.'

Action: The gang moved swiftly and silently. One group, showing a sure knowledge of hydraulic and steam-brake systems, uncoupled the engine and the front two coaches from the rest of the train. The others handcuffed Mills and Whitby, and then ordered them to drive the truncated train a mile up the tracks to Bridego Bridge, which had been carefully marked with strips of white canvas. Then the bandits crashed their way into the locked mail coach with crowbars and pickaxes, herded the post-office workers into a corner and ordered them to 'sit down and be quiet' while they deftly snatched bags,

emptied sorting bins, and grabbed banknotes from smashed-in cupboards. Rapidly, but carefully, they loaded 120 sacks and humped them down over the bridge into trucks 15 feet below.

The operation had taken 15 minutes. In the rear of the stationary, engineless train, post-office workers in their sleek maroon coaches worked on, unknowing and unconcerned.

It was another 45 minutes before an alarm was raised by two young GPO workers who stumbled through wheat fields to Cecil Rawdings' Redborough Farm. But there was no telephone in the farmhouse. So one of them borrowed a bicycle and cycled 1½ miles to the hamlet of Linslade to rouse the village constable, while the other had a cup of tea with Mrs Rawdings, who had thoughtfully put the kettle on.

Dozens of officers from Scotland Yard's Flying Squad quickly reached the scene. Roadblocks were set up in Buckinghamshire and thirteen other counties. Police with tracker dogs scoured the countryside. Railway detectives began combing records of past employees because the 'caper' had all the looks of an inside job. Later in the day, plain-clothes police swarmed through racetrack crowds and shady drinking spots, seeking known 'grasses' (informers). Interpol, the international police organization, was asked to keep an eye out for fences and street-corner money-changers in European capitals.

At week's end, it was still uncertain just how much the raiders had snatched this time. But it was at least $7 million, much of it in old £1 notes, and reward offers from insurance companies already totalled almost $750,000.

© Newsweek, 1963

After reading the text can you put the following events back in their correct order? (Number them from 1 to 11.)

- [ ] The gang members seize the engineer.
- [ ] The engineer stops the train.
- [ ] Tom Miller realizes some of the coaches of the train have gone.
- [ ] The engineer finds that the telephone wires have been cut.
- [ ] The gang members change the green light to a red light.
- [ ] Police block the roads to try and catch the gangsters.
- [ ] The bandits separate the coach containing the money.
- [ ] The engineer prepares to leave the train to phone.
- [ ] One of the workers on the train calls the police.
- [ ] The gang members put the bags into trucks.
- [ ] The gang members force the engineer to drive some of the coaches further along the track.

12
Cows in Calcutta

1

HOLLAND TAKES CALCUTTA COWS BY THE HORNS

Holland has undertaken a daring new project in the developing world. It has agreed to finance the removal of 60,000 cows from the centre of Calcutta.

The costs of this operation are estimated at approximately 19 million Dutch guilders (about £9,500,000).

1.1   The following is an extract from a report in a Dutch newspaper. Read it very
      quickly so as to get a rough idea about the project and the problems involved.

MORE THAN 60,000 milk-
ing cows are being kept
illegally in 2000 sheds in the
slums of Calcutta. Slums
which are already crowded
with three million people.

Add to this a few thousand
stray cows that lie down at
night with the poor people who
sleep in the streets. The tons
of dung produced by the animals prevents any reorganization
in the city. Feeble attempts by
the Indian authorities to provide these slums with elementary services such as street-
fountains, pavements, and a
drainage system have failed.
The drains are blocked by cow-
dung.

Holland has already given
11 million guilders (D.fl.
11,000,000) for the completion
of a number of half-built hospitals and to finance a number
of schools in Calcutta. Now it
wants to contribute to solving
the problem of the cows and to
have them removed to sheds
outside the town, and to end
the black market traffic in
milk. The money is there, but
how much longer will the low-
ing of cows still be heard in
the city centre? Because, if you
touch the Indian cow, you
touch the mystery of India.

Contacts have been made
with the C.M.D.A., an organization involved in the development of the city. The Indians
will do everything themselves.
The Dutch will only provide
the necessary funds. Said the
Indian Ambassador Mr Rasgota: 'We are a big country. We
have our own culture and our
own independent policy; we
want to do things ourselves and
in our own way'.

And a C.M.D.A. official declared: 'You have chosen the
right sort of project. At last it
is not something spectacular,
involving a lot of prestige, such
as the building of a bridge or a
dam.'

However, there is no guarantee whatsoever that the project
will be successful. Not one cow
has been removed so far. Enormous problems are involved in
the acquisition of land outside
the town. The farmers now living in apartments in town and
exploiting their cows in the
slum area are strongly opposed

to the plans. It is their only
source of income. They do not
welcome the idea of having to
rent expensive sheds outside
the town and supplying milk to
the consumers through dairies.
Even the consumers distrust
bottles of pasteurized milk.
They prefer having the cows
milked in front of their very
eyes. And at least they are
sure of getting the milk now.
The Calcutta City authorities
cannot provide more than one
third of the milk needed for its
ten million inhabitants. That is
why the black market exists.

1.2   Can you state very briefly what exactly the Dutch propose to do and what they
      expect from the Indians?

1.3 Can you combine these parts into ten complete sentences again? If necessary you may consult the text.

A Feeble attempts

B More than 60,000 milking-cows are being kept illegally

C And a C.M.D.A. official declared:

D Because, if you

E Said the Indian Ambassador, Mr Rasgota:

F The farmers now living

G Contacts have been made

H There is no guarantee whatsoever that

I Add to this a few thousand stray cows

J Even the consumers

1 with the C.M.D.A., an organization

2 the project will be

3 touch the Indian cow,

4 in 2000 sheds in the slums of Calcutta

5 distrust

6 to provide these slums with elementary services such as

7 that lie down at night with

8 you have chosen

9 we are a big country; we have

10 in apartments in town and exploiting their cows in the slum area

a which are already crowded with three million people.

b the right sort of project.

c street fountains, pavements, and a drainage system have failed.

d involved in the development of the city.

e successful.

f the poor people that sleep in the streets.

g our own culture and our own independent policy.

h are strongly opposed to the plans.

i you touch the mystery of India.

j bottles of pasteurized milk.

1.4 You have combined the above parts into complete sentences; now put them in a logical order without consulting the text again.

1.5 India does a lot to solve its own problems. It also receives aid from all over the world. In the article on p.92 only some contributions are mentioned. Can you specify them in the following table?

	amount	to be used for	where?
aid given in the past	D.fl. £		
aid offered now	D.fl. £		

2 India has got its problems. What about your country? Can you think of a similar world problem or one in your own country or town?

- Agree with your partner(s) on a subject of your choice.
  You may choose one in the list below, or one of your own.
- Draw up a list of possible solutions suggested by all partners, then decide on three of them for further discussion.
- List the advantages and disadvantages of each of them.
- Decide on the solution you prefer.
- Report your findings to other groups. Use the form given by your teacher, which can be completed during the discussion.

Some suggestions.

a We are very wasteful of energy.
b Certain species of animal are threatened with extinction.
c Weather patterns could be changing due to nuclear explosions and the destruction of rain-forests.
d Many people in the world are still illiterate.
e Life in most towns is made almost impossible by the car.
f Women in many countries are taking a more active part in the traditionally male domains of government and business, but their status hasn't really changed.

3 Mr Mohammed Jaheruddin, born in Bangladesh, has lived in Europe for a long time and is keenly interested in Development Aid. He discusses the article in 1.1.

3.1 Listen to the interview. Does Mr Jaheruddin confirm the facts about the situation in Calcutta?

3.2 After seeing Mr Jaheruddin, the interviewer falls ill. A younger colleague had to write the article. His understanding of English was not too good however. Read the article, listen to the tape again (in parts) and mark each part of the article true or false.

Mr Jaheruddin talks about Dutch project

		true	false
a	In an interview Mr Jaheruddin of Bangladesh discussed the Dutch scheme to remove 80,000 cows from the centre of Calcutta.	☐	☐
b	If the black market were abolished the Government could only provide one third of the milk needed.	☐	☐
c	Mr Jaheruddin believes this Dutch scheme will not be successful because all the cows are Holy Cows.	☐	☐
d	Moreover, people prefer to see the milk they will buy coming straight from the cow and are distrustful of bottled milk.	☐	☐
e	Mr Jaheruddin thinks it would be an excellent idea if foreign experts came to carry out the scheme.	☐	☐
f	He said India would provide the money.	☐	☐
g	When asked if keeping cows in the centre of Calcutta was unhygienic he said yes, it was but people did not care about this.	☐	☐

Suggestions for writing assignments

Choose one or more of the following:

a A young European agricultural expert has just arrived in Calcutta. The Director of C.M.D.A., Mr Möitra, has taken him to the centre of the town. Write a short dialogue between this young man and Mr Möitra.

What you see:

poor people sleeping on the pavement
stray cows
a cow-shed, almost hidden from sight
a market-place where people buy milk
a street-fountain that does not work
cow-dung and dirt everywhere

You may use some of the following expressions:

When you are surprised:

Is that so?
Really?
It's unbelievable!

When you draw attention to something:

Look at that, …
Hey, what's this, …
Now watch …

When you suggest something:

Now, if …
Yes, but what about …
Wouldn't it be a good idea if …

Now listen to the actual conversation they had.

b You recently read an article about a project in Bombay, which is being carried out under the supervision of Mr Tragler, an Austrian planning expert. The project aims at building apartment flats for 140 families now living in the slums of Bombay. You think the Dutch money would be better spent on a similar project. At the same time little pieces of land could be bought for the tenants.

Advantages: employment for the poorest, they might grow their own food. Instead of improving the conditions for cows one could help human beings.

Write a short letter to a magazine called *Asiaweek* in which you express your feelings. Think of a suitable headline.

c You read a letter like the one outlined above (b). You disagree with the writer and write a letter to *Asiaweek*. What would your letter be like?

13
Making your own art

1

£75 for Your Story

All our stories were sent in by readers. Do you have a true story, from your own experience? Write and tell us. We pay £75 for every one of your stories accepted.

For other short items and end-of-article 'fillers' we pay readers from £10 upwards.

Send your story to:
Excerpts, Reader's Weekly,
420 Bedford Square,
London
W2X 4AB.

Make sure your name and address appear on all items.

The Editor regrets that he cannot acknowledge or return contributions, or accept responsibility for loss or damage. All payments are made on acceptance.

Changing Your Address?
Please use the coupon on page 214.

Paul read the advertisement in which *Reader's Weekly* invites people to send in stories from their own experience, and he decided to write something about his latest hobby.

He did not particularly want to earn £75, but he thought his experiences might be stimulating for other people who would like to take their minds off the daily routine of their jobs.

The following is his story, which has not been published so far.

No matter what pressure is put on us: Thursday night is always kept free for art.

"We" are a small group of friends who meet in Joe's studio every Thursday night. Joe is a bit of everything. He has to earn his living by teaching, because he cannot afford to be just a painter. He, his wife Helen, and the two youngest of his four children live on a farm, which he renovated himself with the help of a few friends.

In the corner of an old barn he has a small smithy where he also keeps his electric power tools. Here he does all his metal work. In the loft of the barn he now has his studio.

It was John who had persuaded me to come and join them. "It is so nice to paint for a few hours, discuss your work with Joe, or just sit down with a glass of wine and talk about art", he told me. John himself has really got a talent for painting, and I often think it's Joe's secret wish that one day John will give up his job and become a full-time painter.

So, one night I went down to Joe's place and he taught me the first principles of welding, because that's what I had chosen to do. I had always been fascinated when I had watched welders fuse pieces of metal together hiding their faces in masks to protect their eyes from the blinding sparks of light.

I don't think I'll ever make a great artist, but the making of my first object out of metal scraps gave me enormous satisfaction. Friends and relatives could not agree on whether it represented a hen or a platform from which missiles are launched into space, but that did not bother me at all. For me it was Mrs B, down the road, weeding her garden!

Joe was very encouraging. Very tactfully he told me that I really needed more practice in drawing, and that's how he managed to get me up to the loft to join the others.

They had just started using a live model and after some hesitation I followed their example. In the next few weeks I made six or seven pictures of her in charcoal, but I have to admit that no two of them were similar and none looked like the model. I ended up by restricting myself to drawing the chair in which she sat. Joe very sympathetically said I had made a lot of progress.

The next step was painting in oils. "A real challenge," Joe had said. I acquired the materials I needed and gradually Joe taught me how to mix the colours and to use my brushes or knife.

At home I now have two new paintings hanging on the wall. They're not very good, but I made them myself. For all the world I would not have missed the fun I had in struggling with the paint, the brushes, and the canvas!

2   Discuss the following questions with your partner(s). If necessary, go back to the text.

2.1   Paul wrote this story, because:

a He was afraid he had worked too hard and needed a cure.   ☐

b He wanted to stimulate other people to take up the same hobby.   ☐

c *Reader's Weekly* had invited him to write something about his latest hobby.   ☐

d He wanted to earn £75.   ☐

Tick the right answer(s).

2.2   Five people are mentioned. What facts are given about each of them?

facts about:	Joe	John	Paul	model	Mrs B
profession					
leisure time					
family					
house					
skill in art					
………					
………					

So, who do we know least about?
Who do we know most about?
Is this also the person we now know best?

2.3   Paul tried three kinds of art.

a Which order did he do them in?
b Why did he do each of them?
c Where did he work?
d What did he make and what materials did he use?

Use the table which your teacher will give you to take down some notes.

£75 for Your Story

Reader's Weekly tries to get its readers to do something by promising money.
What does the magazine want them to do?
How does it say this?

This was said:	Why?
Do you have a true story? Write and tell us.	To get people to write their stories and tell *Reader's Weekly* about them.
Changing your address? Please use the coupon on page 214.	To get people to inform *Reader's Weekly* about their new address.

Now think of John, Paul, Joe, and the model in the story above. Can you guess
who said what, to whom, and why?

This was said:	Who said it?	To whom?	To get him/her to …
'What about turning up the stove? I'm freez-ing, brrr!'			
'Why don't you join us?'			
'I would practise drawing now, and afterwards go back to welding.'			
'Can you show me some good brushes? Oh, yes, and I need a canvas and some paint.'			

3   You are now going to hear the first part of an interview with another person
interested in art. You will not understand everything but there are a few things
you could find out by listening just once:

a The profession of the person interviewed.
b His identity (name, address, and so on).
c His most important hobby.
d Does he think he's good at his job?
e Is his hobby relaxing or hard work?

Take down your answers (brief notes) on a form like this.

Do not worry if you cannot complete it immediately, but keep entering notes as
you listen to the text for the other assignments.

PERSONAL FILE

---

1 INTERVIEWEE

Name: .... Address: ....

Male/female: .... Country: ....

Profession: .... Age: ....

Hobbies: ....

....

Physical fitness: ....

Financial situation: ....

Any relatives mentioned? ....

Any friends mentioned? ....

Social life (clubs / organisations): ....

Character: optimist ☐   pessimist ☐

            confident ☐   shy ☐

            believes in what he says ☐   indifferent ☐

---

2 INTERVIEW

Subject: ....

Nature of interview: general ☐   specific ☐

                      interesting ☐   not interesting ☐

                      easy to follow ☐ difficult ☐

4 Now listen again to the interview while it is played in parts. Do the following assignments:

4.1 How does he use his free time? (Tick off appropriate boxes.)

	sports												travel	art
	football	rugby	hockey	baseball	netball	tennis	walking	horse-riding	swimming	climbing	car-racing	cycling		
actively (doing)														
watching/looking at														

4.2 Listen to part of the tape again and fill in the missing words. Make sure you get the exact words on the tape.

'… on the ……… of ……… house there should be either the best art or ……… art. And if you can't ………, as I can't, because ……… that I'm a ………, then the ……… best thing is ……… .'

4.3 Why is art important for him?

a It's a therapy. (He's overworked by teaching.) ☐

b It takes his mind off his job. ☐

c He has not told us. ☐

4.4 What does he say about making art and teaching? Draw the correct arrows:
← or →

	paid for	
	unpaid	
art	exhausting	teaching
	not like having a beer or sitting on the beach	

4.5 Which of the following statements are true and which are false?

	true	false
a Making a sculpture takes him months.	☐	☐
b He usually works in stone.	☐	☐
c The sculpture has to be cut down from blocks, often a yard high.	☐	☐
d He works with chisels and mallets.	☐	☐
e He never uses power tools.	☐	☐
f He uses sandpaper.	☐	☐
g He never makes a drawing before he starts working on a sculpture.	☐	☐
h Sometimes, when the sculpture is finished, all the work is wasted because the material splits.	☐	☐

4.6 In what order did he do the various activities? And why?

Activities	Reasons why he took them up
1	....
2	....
3	....

4.7 Why has he not worked in metal?

a His studio at home has not got the machinery. ☐

b He has not got a studio at home. ☐

c He can use somebody else's machinery, but he prefers to work at home. ☐

4.8 Can you tick which parts of the body he mentions?

a	backbone	☐	j	back	☐
b	hip	☐	k	brain	☐
c	jaw	☐	l	breast or chest	☐
d	joint	☐	m	buttocks	☐
e	pelvis	☐	n	hair	☐
f	rib	☐	o	head	☐
g	shoulder	☐	p	navel	☐
h	skull	☐	q	neck	☐
i	abdomen	☐	r	waist	☐

5   Look at these two works of art: *Alarm! Florentine Soldier* by Michelangelo, (1500), and *Reclining Figure* by Henry Moore, (1969).

'The figure is the basis of all sculpture …'

a Is what is said by Henry Moore true of this sculpture?
b Which parts of the human body do you see in the drawing of the Florentine
   Soldier? Why is it called 'Alarm'?
c What differences do you notice between the two figures?